how to start a home-based

Recording Studio Business

HOME-BASED BUSINESS SERIES

how to start a home-based

Recording Studio Business

Joe Shambro

Guilford, Connecticut

Text designed by Sheryl P. Kober

Library of Congress Cataloging-in-Publication Data

Shambro, Joe.
  How to start a home-based recording studio business / Joe Shambro.
    p. cm.
  ISBN 978-0-7627-6124-1
  1. Music trade—Vocational guidance. 2. Sound recording
industry—Vocational guidance. I. Title.
  ML3795.S412 2011
  781.49068′1—dc22
                         2010039751

Printed in the United States of America

10 9 8 7 6 5 4 3 2 1

Dedicated to everyone who's ever dreamed of starting their own business, and worked hard to achieve that dream—whether they found success or failure in the end—including my hard-working parents, Jim and Nancy.

Special thanks to my patient and experienced editorial team at Globe Pequot Press for helping this occasionally-disorganized and technically-oriented audio engineer become an even better writer, and make a fantastic book in the process (especially Mike Urban, whose help and sage advice was invaluable, for now and the future).

Contents

Introduction

In the fall of 2003, I took out two small business loans and started my own business. My background was in live sound reinforcement and live recording, and I'd made a name for myself by producing some really high-quality recordings. Somewhere along the line I got the fine idea that I wanted to open my own studio—and record bigger, better, and higher-paying clients. I was so excited the day I applied for my first loan; all I could think about was getting to Guitar Center and picking up the gear I had chosen to start off my studio. I was excited to have new toys to play with!

A couple of short months later, I had just opened my home-based recording studio to the world. I was full of hope and dreams and all the other stuff small businesses rely on to get by. Right after I opened I made contact with a very promising client, and I was waiting for him to come to my home studio to have a consultation meeting. It was one of my first serious client meetings and I was extremely nervous, as you might expect.

My studio was in a chic urban loft complex that I could barely afford, chosen specifically for double-duty as living and recording space, with my control room in a spare bedroom connected to my large, open living room, which was doubling as my live recording room. I had prepared the night before with a playlist of my best demo material and even ran the vacuum sweeper to make sure my studio looked its best. I prepared myself to answer every potential question. The client showed up somewhat late (the old joke of "rock and roll time," a built-in, automatic tardiness of anywhere between fifteen and thirty minutes when dealing with musicians, is actually painfully accurate) and I enthusiastically buzzed him up. Our pre-meeting conversations had been great, and I felt like we were a perfect match. His band sounded great, and with some of my production magic, their album could be one of the best projects I'd ever worked on.

After opening my door and exchanging pleasantries, we walked into my studio—at the time, a very modest setup that included a small but capable Pro Tools interface, some good microphone preamps, and the latest Apple iMac, a machine with great processing power for the time. He froze completely, the disappointment in his face substantial—even the unnecessary eyeliner this 20-something-year-old man was wearing couldn't hide his true feelings.

"Um . . . where's the mixing board and all that kind of . . . stuff?" he asked, waving his hand dismissively at the places in my studio where he envisioned the equipment should be.

"Well, this is it. Welcome to my control room. How about we take a listen to some—"

"I'm sorry, I . . . " he said, cutting me off mid-sentence. "I just thought I was coming to a real recording studio. Sorry. I don't think this is going to work out."

And with that, he turned around and walked out the door. I was devastated; certainly, it was a demoralizing experience for a young business owner in the first months of business. At worst, the sinking feeling I got from the experience was equivalent to meeting a perfect-sounding date on the Internet, having great, hours-long phone conversations, and then finally meeting after weeks of anticipation only to go home afraid to ever meet someone online again. I wasn't prepared for somebody to look at my hard-earned studio and reject it. I probably sat on the couch feeling sorry for myself for days afterward.

Losing this client hurt, especially because it had nothing to do with my skill as an audio engineer. He looked at my modest home studio and assumed that because I was missing what he envisioned as the stereotypical recording studio experience, my work wasn't worth his time or money. I knew better, but it still hurt. It was a big challenge to overcome, and I wish I could tell you that this was the only time this happened. Unfortunately, being a home-based business presents many challenges, this being just one of them.

Fortunately for you, times have changed drastically. The recording industry has been turned upside down by the DIY ethic of today's independent musicians. Studios themselves aren't what they used to be, and the expectations of most technologically savvy musicians have been realigned to reflect this. While big mixing boards and racks of outboard gear (especially those beautiful SSL and Neve consoles) make fantastic recordings in capable hands, small home-based studios can produce quality work with carefully selected, affordable gear. It's never been a better time to jump into the world of studio recording, especially as a home-based business. That being said, you've got some awfully stiff competition. In today's economy, many bands are finding it just as easy to record their music in their own home studios, using any of the plethora of equipment priced within reach of most working musicians.

As time went on, running my business presented a whole new set of challenges. I'm confident enough to admit I made some big mistakes. The first year out, I was clueless about good financial management. And the business plan I had written? It wasn't worth the paper I printed it on. I also completely screwed up my taxes. I screwed them up so bad that I didn't even file them. How's that for giving up? (And, as the IRS knows, I took care of it later on.)

I learned more and more about the hard work ethic it requires to run your own business day in and day out.

A year into it, I had completely changed everything—from where my business was located, to how I managed my bookkeeping and taxes, and taking more time to see the details through to the end. I was giving my clients the best experience they could ask for—efficiency and value, along with very high-quality work. It took time, but I had finally hit my stride, and it took a year of cluelessly running my business before I was able to realize I had to take time to do it right. I started over, rewriting my business plan and sticking to it. I had a more realistic vision of where I needed to be. And by taking time to learn some very valuable lessons the hard way, I became a much better businessperson.

While it may seem really easy, running a home based business is actually very, very hard work. In your home environment you've got distractions—a lot of them, especially if you've got kids at home. Being unable to separate "home" from "work" is another issue you'll need to find a way to overcome. However, the rewards are well worth it. Being able to set your own schedule and call the shots on your business's day-to-day operations is worth all of the frustration that will come from running this business. It's also potentially heartbreaking when things don't go your way. Trust me, I've felt this, too.

I've written this book to be the reference I never had when opening my home-based recording studio. I'm very confident that you'll be able to use this book to guide you through the extremely rough terrain that comes with starting your own business. And you'll be able to use the solid foundation that this book gives you to keep your business running soundly (and hopefully profitably).

So, strap in and enjoy the ride—whether you're going full-time or part-time, opening a small project studio or a major commercial-grade tracking facility, you're in for a journey filled with hard work, heartache, and stress like you've never felt before. In the end, whether your business succeeds or not, you'll know you gave it your best shot.

Let's get started.

01 So You Want to Start a Home-Based Recording Studio

Why Start a Home-Based Recording Studio?

A few years ago the idea of a fully functional recording studio inside some-one's home was a key component in most rock-star fantasies, but in reality this concept was far out of reach both financially and logistically. In order to have a studio worthy of attracting paying clients (and capable of churn-ing out professional-quality work), you needed to dedicate two things most people in this industry don't have: money and space. Think about it: To have a studio capable of recording twenty-four tracks simultaneously, you'd need a mixing board, lots of outboard gear (compressors, gates, effects, and equal-izers), and analog or digital multitrack recorders, not to mention the space for your clients to set up and record properly—including isolation rooms for vocals and acoustic instruments. Even buying middle-of-the-road equipment, you were looking at several thousand dollars to even get started. How the times have changed!

Now, a spare bedroom, empty garage, or basement can easily be turned into a functional, world-class studio with a relatively low investment. Record-ing equipment of such high quality has never before been available at such reasonable prices, allowing smaller studios access to industry-standard qual-ity at a fraction of what you'd have paid ten or fifteen years ago. You're not just limited to simple two- or four-track recording either; we're talking as many channels as you could possibly need, often in 24-bit, 96-kHz resolution. If you're a good recording engineer with confidence in your skills, working from home should pose no limitation to producing quality work, especially given the tools you have access to with a modest budget. In fact, some great albums by multiplatinum artists were recorded in their own home studios. And many started out as rough sketches made by the band in their bedrooms (or, as is increasingly common, on the tour bus) with what's now considered consumer-grade equipment.

Aside from the obvious benefits of being your own boss (more on this challenging scenario later), the biggest benefit of running your business from home is the advantage of not having the high overhead of a full-on commercial operation. This means lower prices for your clients, which translates to more business and better profits for you. Buying or renting a space, building it out to your specifications, maintaining it, and paying utilities can add up very quickly—easily to the half-million-dollar mark (or more) if you choose to go with top-notch acoustic treatment. If you're already paying for housing (rent, mortgage, barter, whatever the situation may be) and you have extra space, using this space for your business makes perfect sense.

Is Self-Employment for You?

Someone once said, "What's the greatest benefit of being self-employed? Calling my old boss every day at noon to tell him I just woke up." It's a funny line, but I guarantee the person who wittily came up with that joke wasn't telling the whole story. You see, self-employment, even on the days you can sleep in until noon, is very hard work. According to the results of Gallup Work and Education Surveys done from 2006 to 2009, almost half of self-employed Americans work between forty-four and sixty hours per week, going well beyond the standard forty-hour workweek followed by most workers in private companies; in fact, over a quarter of all self-employed people reported working over sixty hours per week. That's a lot of extra time to put in, and it may seem daunting, but remember one thing: You're doing everything. You are your business. You'll be handling marketing, payroll, accounting, and providing the actual product or service your business offers—a lot of responsibility!

For all the hard work that comes with running your own business, you've also got some distinct advantages. Want to always be home when the kids get dropped off from school? You can be. Want to travel, spend time with friends and family, and generally enjoy the benefits of setting your own schedule? That's something you can work toward, too—but remember, it won't come easy. Running a business means a lot more responsibility than you may have had previously, simply because it's necessary to wear many different hats at the same time, until it's economically feasible to bring in other employees.

The biggest problem for most self-employed people is giving up the financial stability and benefits that come from a typical job. After thirty-four-and-a-half years,

Interns

Interns are one solution that many recording studios rely on to provide quality help at no cost. Interns are usually college students or older, who have a working knowledge of the recording industry, and are eager to get some hands-on time in hopes of independently securing paid sessions in the future. Whether or not you hire interns is up to you, but if you treat them right (and give them plenty of hands-on time), they can become very valuable members of your team.

my father retired from a security job at a steel mill with fantastic benefits—health insurance, retirement savings, a credit union with low-interest home and auto loans, paid vacation, not to mention a reliable middle-class paycheck. It was a job he didn't particularly like, but he did it because it was stable and allowed him to support his family well. Being without this reliable paycheck would have been extremely hard for him, as it is for many people, especially in today's economic climate. Being self-employed means you'll be single-handedly responsible for meeting your financial needs. If the business does poorly, you don't make any money. You'll also have to find your own benefits—and as a self-employed person, those benefits can cost a lot of money.

Health insurance is one of those benefits that you will likely lose if you become self-employed; many employers provide health insurance as a free or reduced-cost benefit to their employees. Finding your own health coverage can be a challenge and downright expensive. In fact when I first became self-employed, I went without health insurance and was uninsured from 2002 through 2007 when I took a contract job that allowed me access to health benefits. I simply couldn't find any affordable health coverage at the time, and having a small pre-existing condition didn't help matters. (For those in the same situation, it's important to note that you can include pre-existing medical conditions into your new coverage if there's no gap in coverage.) The idea of being uninsured is scary to many people, especially those with special medical issues that require prescriptions and frequent check-ups, not to mention the devastating costs of an accident or long-term illness. Managing your finances is another very important part of running your own business. We'll talk about it in more detail later, but managing the business's financial needs can be one of the most daunting and time-consuming things you have to tackle. Keep in mind that being "the boss" doesn't mean you can reach into your takings and spend money at any time; just like any other business, you'll need to pay your expenses and taxes while also taking care of yourself.

Meet Your New Boss—YOU

When I first made the decision to pursue a career as a self-employed person, I had lofty expectations. While there was something really attractive about setting my own schedule, there was equal attraction to the romantic idea of being lazy whenever I wanted. It wasn't long before I realized that the actual lifestyle of the self-employed is nowhere near the lifestyle of the independently wealthy—something I somehow didn't realize. Being your own boss is hard work, and it takes a remarkable amount of discipline. As mentioned earlier, being self-employed is quite a challenge; it requires a great deal of patience, an attention to detail like you've never imagined, and a Zen-like tolerance for the unexpected. That's not even touching on the complicated financial realities of being self-employed.

What does it mean to be your own boss? Quite simply, it's all about discipline. In your old life, chances are you showed up, worked your job, and went home. You did whatever it was that you did, did it well, and collected a paycheck. Not any more! The clients are your customers and their needs will always dictate your actions, ultimately, but you're also going to have to learn to manage yourself as if you're managing an employee. When you're the boss, time management is the most critical aspect of your workday. Running your own business will require you to make plenty of time for all of the necessary maintenance that a business requires, and because you're the boss, you're going to have to crack the proverbial whip to get yourself going.

Consistency is one of the most important things you'll need to remember when it comes to managing yourself. Making a schedule, sticking to it, and meeting your weekly goals is the best way to make sure you're running your business successfully.

Just being a good recording engineer isn't enough. You might be able to turn out a great product in record time, but there's a lot you need to do behind the scenes. Keep in mind that your business will also need you, as the owner, to:

- advertise and work on marketing efforts, including social and industry networking;
- maintain legal standards, including taxes and local business regulations;

- navigate the delicate politics and standards of the always-evolving music industry;
- dedicate time to customer service, including time to fix jobs gone bad; and
- manage your business finances, including invoicing and paying bills.

Remember what we just said about how most self-employed workers put in long hours? I'm sure you can see why. If this is your new full-time job, you'll have a lot of weight to carry. Are you considering going only part-time? That's great, too, but you're still a business. The rules don't change just because you're only running a part-time studio. You're still responsible for making sure that your business is legal and your finances are in order, no matter what. In chapter 4, we'll get into these necessities in greater detail.

Checklist: Are You Ready to Be Your Own Boss?

So, do you think you're ready to be your own boss? Sure, it's exciting—I remember how good it felt to go to work for myself. But it's also a lot of hard work, and it requires a certain amount of discipline to accomplish. How do you know if you're ready to be your own boss?

❒   Can you work well under pressure, with little guidance or extra hands?

❒   Can you figure out precisely how much you need to get by, and how you'll leverage your business to (hopefully) bring it in for you?

❒   Do you feel confident in your abilities, not only to offer a quality product and service, but in your ability to manage a business?

❒   Can you stay on-task, despite always having the distractions of home?

If you answered yes to all of these, then congratulations—you've got the right mindset to take a stab at your own business.

Balancing Work AND Family

As should now be clear, running your own recording studio is a big undertaking. It's not just putting your engineering skills to the test, it's running a business, too. If you're working a traditional job at this time, you've probably got a good handle on how to divide your time between work and home. It's easy. You clock out at the end of the day and leave work behind. But running your own business is a new thrill like you never expected—it will easily become an all-consuming, twenty-four-hour worry. The success or failure of your new venture is entirely your responsibility, and this adds considerable stress to your daily life. It can also start affecting those closest to you: your family.

Balancing work and family is one of the most important things you'll need to learn when starting your own business, especially one that's located in your own home. While you might be tempted to funnel every ounce of your energy and every second of your time into your new venture, you'll need to set up boundaries. Yes, you'll likely put in more hours per week than you did at your previous job, especially when things get going full speed. But remember: What good is the extra work if you can't make time for what's important in your life also? Take it from someone who's been in your shoes: Find a good balance between the time you spend working, the time you spend with those you care about, and the time you spend doing things you enjoy.

How the Industry Has Changed

First and foremost, you need to have a keen understanding of how this process has changed over the years. Knowing the basics of the professional music industry isn't a bonus—it's something you will be expected to provide, from your first client onward. Even if your client doesn't have any aspirations beyond the local scene, upholding industry-standard practices and policies within your studio will only help further your studio's reputation as a professional, industry-standard resource in your local community.

The music business as a whole has seen a lot of change in the last few years. Nowhere else has there been better evidence of this than in the home recording studio. Independent music is the way of the future—just look at how much money the major labels have lost recently—and with a small recording studio, you're in a great position to help this growing market. As a small operation, you're unlikely to attract much commercial interest from larger-label artists until you've established yourself as an engineer. The vast majority of your clientele will be independent musicians coming to you to record demos (mainly for use in booking shows or to take to a larger, more expensive commercial studio later on) or full-length albums that they intend to release for both promotion and profit.

One of the game-changing realities of the music business is digital distribution. In the past, when an artist wanted to release an album to the masses, they had to go through a traditional channel: the record label. With the exception of a few mail-order companies (and many of those, too, were controlled by record labels), artists had very little affordable access to recording studios, duplication, and physical product distribution. In order to put out a record on your own, you had to be either very well connected or extremely wealthy—sometimes both. Record labels controlled everything: the recording process, how an artist was promoted, where an artist's albums were sold, and how much money the artist made for his or her work. Getting signed to a label was the be-all end-all for most performing musicians.

In the late 1990s, the playing field started to level slightly through two major revolutions. One, recording technology began to get a lot cheaper, and more successful mid- and small-sized operations started to offer more affordable recording, mastering, and duplication—especially on CD. Two, the Internet, for the first time, put the same promotional and distribution channels of the major labels into the hands of independent musicians. These days a band can, theoretically, start with nothing and work their way up to being successful through their own hard work and hustle, using many of the same avenues that previously only major labels had access to.

Are Your Skills Up to Par?

When talking to musicians who've worked with recording studios in the past, one of the most frustrating experiences that many of them expressed was working with an engineer who didn't have the skills necessary to pull off a full-scale production. Unfortunately, that's a big problem with the digital revolution of most recording studios. While I don't want to discourage you from following your dreams, keep in mind that your skills may need some polishing before you begin taking on paying clients. Many of today's software packages offer pre-sets and plug-ins that can give you a fairly professional-sounding mix with very little work on your part. Unfortunately, just being able to use these tools to your satisfaction may not necessarily indicate that you're ready to move on to accepting paying clients.

Being a good audio engineer requires a deep familiarity with the tools, procedures, and technical theories that make good recordings possible. That being said, playing everything "by the book" is one of the biggest downfalls of aspiring sound engineers, too. I see a lot of this when working with new engineers—and it's very frustrating, especially when I see good clients trusting their complex work to someone who doesn't understand the basics. Look at it this way: Just because there's a common set of rules for certain situations doesn't mean that those rules apply to everything. You'll have to learn to utilize your knowledge and skills in every possible situation.

So how can you tell if your skills are up to tackling a commercial recording studio situation? Here's a list of basic skills—compiled with the help of fellow professional-level audio engineers—that you should be proficient in before considering yourself open for business. Remember, going into a complicated session without the knowledge to bail yourself out of just about any situation can cost you time and money, not to mention a gigantic hit to your reputation.

Audio Engineering: Basic Skill Requirements

- **Signal Flow.** Knowledge of basic electrical engineering concepts, including gain structure, balanced and unbalanced connections, and simple cable repair. Working knowledge of phase relationships.
- **Software.** Professional-level mastery of both Avid Pro Tools and Apple Logic Pro (at a bare minimum); 98 percent of projects will require one of these two suites.
- **Microphones.** Working knowledge of polar patterns, element types, and appropriate applications, including stereo microphone techniques (X/Y, ORTF, NOS, A/B, etc.).
- **Outboard Equipment.** Even if you're planning on staying in-the-box for mixing and mastering, you'll still need working knowledge of the signal flow and operation of microphone preamplifiers, compressors, gates, equalizers, and other processing gear as necessary.
- **Editing Techniques.** Fluency with linear audio editing (splicing, blending, fades, normalization); Auto-Tune and Melodyne pitch correction; aesthetically appropriate dynamics control, including compression, gating, expanders, and limiters; and extensive knowledge of how to appropriately apply equalization.

- **Mixing Techniques.** You should be able to achieve high-quality stereo mixes with depth, character, and richness to your clients' exact specifications. Expertise with the aesthetics of a quality mix is essential, and being able to dissect a mix to diagnose and repair phase anomalies and sloppy editing is mandatory.

Your Most Important Tool: Your Ears

Hearing conservation is one of the most ignored topics for audio engineers. It might not seem like a subject you need to pay attention to this early in the game, but if you want a long, prosperous career in music production, protecting your hearing is very, very important—that's why you're reading this in the first chapter, before you dig in to the studio-building process. While we obsess over our microphone and racks of equipment that look fancy and sound great, the most valuable and important piece of equipment that we all have—and need—is our ears. We only get one pair. Unlike most of our other equipment, we can't just call over to Guitar Center or Sweetwater and order a new set of eardrums, or swap out our auditory nerves for a fresh pair. Hearing loss has somehow become both a running joke and bragging right among musicians and engineers, but it's no laughing matter. Constant unprotected exposure to loud sounds can, over time, make your hearing less sensitive and less accurate, not to mention the constant ringing of tinnitus that can develop. In extreme cases there's potential for profound hearing loss that can affect your normal day-to-day life as well as completely end your career as a musician or recording engineer.

Keep in mind one simple rule: Hearing loss comes from extended exposure. For a full eight-hour workday, a constant 85 decibels is the most you should be exposed to, unprotected. Think that sounds like a lot of leverage? Think again. A busy city street can clock in at around 80 decibels; a band playing at full-on volume can come near to 120 decibels. Today's high-definition studio monitors can easily push close to that, so you're not completely safe in your control room, either; at 120 decibels, you're only safe for seven-and-a-half-minutes-worth of exposure.

Fortunately, there are many options to keep your ears healthy. First, consider investing in a small sound pressure level (SPL) meter. These can cost less than $50—in fact, I've recently begun using an iPhone application that does a rather good job of giving me a baseline reading of my SPL exposure, especially on long mixing sessions. Second, invest in some good earplugs. Avoid foam-type earplugs; while these protect your hearing well, they do so by blocking out sound waves as a whole, resulting in a muffled sound with very little mid- or high-end information. Instead try earplugs that filter the sound, giving you a full-spectrum frequency response, only with reduced volume. You can purchase a pair for under $20 from popular brands such as Etymotic and Mack's—look for earplugs labeled as "musicians' earplugs." For around $150, companies such as Future Sonics, Sensaphonics, and Westone can make custom-fit, filtered earplugs that provide excellent isolation and optimum sound quality—a small investment when you're constantly exposed to loud sounds.

Prevention and awareness are the keys to avoiding hearing loss. If you're leveraging your future on being able to maintain a long, healthy career making people's recordings sound as good as possible, you owe it to yourself to consider protecting your most valuable asset.

Envisioning Your Business

While it may seem redundant to name a chapter "Envisioning Your Business"—after all, if you didn't want to open a recording studio, you wouldn't have bought this book—a recording studio business could take many potential forms. Knowing exactly what you want to do, and making a plan as to how you'll pull it all off will save you time, money, and frustration. Do you want to be a small hip-hop production facility, or do you want to record full bands? How will you stand out from the local competition? And how will your business perform its day-to-day functions? This is what truly envisioning your business is all about. Just deciding what you're going to do isn't enough—you have to figure out the details long before you open your doors to your first client.

Who Needs You?

Most people who get into the recording studio business do so because of music. I'm assuming you have a serious enjoyment of music (and if not, you'll need to develop one as soon as possible) and hopefully a passion for every aspect of the production of music. That being said, most of your customers will come from the music business. They won't be the most profitable projects at first, but your core customer base will come from local musicians needing demos, recordings for release digitally or via CD, or for Internet-based promotional purposes. As your business and résumé grow, you'll probably find more and more customers coming from outside your local area to record, especially if your studio offers something that their local studios can't (more on this in chapter 6).

Even with a love for all things musical, basing an entire business and financial future on working with musicians can be a daunting and patience-stretching process. Musicians don't always have a lot of money to spend, so keep this in mind when working your way up the recording industry ladder. Unfortunately for you, you'll also be starting at the bottom of the ladder, regardless of how good your skills are (or how good you perceive them to be). Established bands will almost always want to partner with more established studios, so you'll need to find ways to set yourself apart from the pack. While I rarely, if ever, advocate giving away freebies to your customers, local musicians are always willing recipients of charity, and that can only help your promotional efforts if it's something you can afford to do as a promotional tool (but don't make a habit of it). Building a good rapport with your local musicians is almost always a necessary step toward developing a good customer base (see chapter 9 for more information on how to use pro bono work to your advantage).

While working with music will probably be your primary focus, don't forget to keep in mind one potentially profitable avenue: corporate work. If you're like most people in the music business, you're rolling your eyes at the idea of becoming a corporate sellout, but don't be so quick to judge. If there's one thing I've learned in my years of self-employment, it's that the concept of "selling out" is never such a bad thing; in fact, selling out can mean the difference between being open for business next month or not.

Corporate clients can come in many forms. It's not always the most exciting work, but one of the best assets of most corporate clients is that they actually pay their bills on time. It's no secret that many small recording studios survive mainly on corporate work—it's generally easy work, and it pays well. Most of the time, you'll be doing music beds (sometimes referred to as "elevator music") or voice-over recording for training videos, telephone "on hold" audio, or audio for television and radio advertisements. Sometimes you'll get lucky and your corporate work will meet in the middle with your love of music. Some of my most profitable, enjoyable, and résumé-building jobs have come from corporate clients in the media industry. Being prepared, and willing, to service these customers will make a huge difference in not only your bottom line, but on your résumé as well.

What Kind of Studio Are You?

Like many other businesses, choosing a specialization can both help your business and save you considerable money in your setup costs. We've talked about the fact that most of your business will come from the music industry, so let's focus on meeting the needs of those clients first.

The first type of studio you might consider opening is a **general-purpose recording studio,** suitable for everything from full bands to soloists to simple voice-over recording. These studios usually require at least one "live room" space— a room large enough for recording, at minimum, a full drum set. You'll also need space for at least one isolated area for vocal and acoustic instrument recording, along with your control area. These general purpose studios require more space than any of the specialized types of studios we'll cover later, but they're also the most versatile and potentially profitable, because you'll be able to take any type of client that comes your way. Obviously, the adapting of space for this large a studio is very hard if you're in a small home without much extra room. Depending on the acoustic quality of your space (and a lot of this depends on the work you've personally done to make the acoustics favorable), you might be able to get by with one recording room for all of these purposes. However, depending on your skills, resources, and most importantly, what type of music you enjoy best, you may decide to specialize in a specific type of recording studio.

Keep in mind: Just as with any business, it'll take you a long time to develop your customer base, and being specialized may be an impediment to early success. If you want to focus on the one thing you know well, don't let this deter you, but be prepared for a potentially longer-than-preferable wait before you start turning a profit.

The most common specialization is for hip-hop artists. These studios don't need very much in the way of live recording space, because most hip-hop artists rely on electronic samples and "beats" to supplement live vocals. One good-quality isolation room is plenty. Outfitting a good **hip-hop studio** generally involves spending a good portion of your budget on samplers and keyboards. You'll need less in the way of microphones. Generally two top-quality vocal microphones will be more than enough. Why two? One microphone isn't always perfect for every voice. Some voices have characteristics that work best with certain microphone types, so consider keeping two high-quality yet contrasting microphones at your disposal as a hip-hop engineer. One condenser, such as the Neumann TLM103 or AKG C414, and one dynamic microphone, such as the Heil PR40 or Shure SM7 is a good place to start. You'll find that these two microphones will suit the vast majority of your hip-hop clientele. You'll also need a high-quality microphone preamp to pair with your microphones. From there, the rest of the equipment is much the same as with any regular studio; you're simply bypassing the multiple inputs and larger space necessary for full-band situations.

Another type of specialized studio is a **mixing-only studio.** Mixing studios are highly focused in that they only mix audio after the recording has been completed at another facility. Many artists, especially top-tier artists, will have their material recorded in one studio, and mixed in another. Being a mix engineer is different than being a recording engineer (in your home studio, chances are you'll be doing both jobs most of the time), and requires a little more finesse and patience. Your job is to balance all parts, perform linear editing, and add effects to make the preferred aesthetic of the song a reality. These studios many times don't feature any live recording space; if they do, it's only a small isolation room with capabilities to record small overdubs if necessary. Mixing studios can be surprisingly profitable; many mixing engineers I know are able to command high hourly rates. But if you're thinking of going that route, keep in mind your established competition. Being a mixing-only studio usually means you'll need to be compatible with every file format that comes your way and every delivery method a potential client will need—Pro Tools and Logic being the two most popular. You'll also need to be able to accept files delivered in multitrack format via hard drive (the most common) and drop them into the mixing suite of your choice. You'll spend a lot more of your budget on plug-ins and outboard equipment, but this will be offset by the smaller amount of money you'll spend on your recording space.

Producing versus Engineering

As a soon-to-be-self-employed studio owner, you'll be asked to wear the hat of both producer and engineer for most of your clients. The advantage here is that you'll be in total control of the studio process with your clients. Aside from keeping yourself sane by having fewer people with their hands in the project, you'll be able to micro-manage your schedule even better when working on extended-length projects. Knowing how to be both a good producer and engineer are key to your success, because most of the time your clients can't afford (and really won't need) both roles filled by different people.

So what's the difference between producing and engineering? Producers tend to be musicians themselves with a firm background in composition and performance. They take the ideas the band has and polish them, helping with every aspect of the recording process, including finishing lyrics, improving individual instrumental parts, and enhancing the band's performance as a whole. They're an invaluable part of the studio process, especially for complicated projects. Engineers, on the other hand, are the technical brain and muscle of the process. A producer tells the engineer what he or she wants, and the engineer uses the technological tools at their disposal to make it happen. In your smaller, home-based operation, most of your clients will require you to play both parts and do it well.

Some clients may wish to bring in an external producer to supplement your work as an engineer. This move is very common for larger-scale clients, although many good producers are also good engineers, too. Generally, a producer is the one who works closely with the band to actualize the band's material and give direction to the engineer on what needs to be done to achieve the finished product. While this may seem redundant for some clients, a good producer can lend a great deal of insight and allow you to remain focused on the technical process of making a good recording. Don't take it personally if a band decides to change course during the recording process and bring in a producer; if they're keeping you around as engineer that lends testament to your skills, even if theirs need some polishing.

Understanding the Studio Process

Congratulations, you've got your first client. What now?

Learning an effective, time-efficient way of running your business is very important. While you might be tempted to bring in your clients, set them up, hit record, and let the music play, it'll save you a lot of time, money, and frustration if you have a plan. Standardizing your studio process is the quickest way to make sure your resources are being used in the most efficient way possible, and that your clients are getting the most out of their dollar—something that will almost always help repeat business.

Typically bands need a surprising amount of guidance in their creative process. Being a good musician isn't always enough: A band that can play songs well in a rehearsal space or on a live stage can easily be intimidated in the studio and completely choke, costing them lots of money on overdubs and wasted recording time. And, yes, I know what you're thinking, even if you won't admit it. It may sound like a good thing for you if a client wastes money on extra session time, but remember what I said about most musicians being broke. You don't want the client to run out of money before the project is done, or risk releasing an inferior product with your name on it.

When starting work with a new client, I typically schedule at least two preproduction meetings (you may wish to do things differently, but hopefully my process can help point you in the right direction). I ask the band to come as a whole and to bring demo recordings of the material they wish to record with me. I also have each member of the band bring at least two tracks that they like by other bands, in terms of style and engineering. The demos can be a live recording, rehearsal recording, or a demo done at another studio. (If your client doesn't have any existing demo material available—because that's what you're going to be helping with—have your first meeting at one of the client's live shows or at a rehearsal session where you can hear the material firsthand.)

Take a listen to the material with the band and then ask them for their vision. They might have a radically different idea about how their demos sound versus how they want their finished product to sound. It's up to you to absorb this and try to take them as close to their final goal as possible. Next listen to the examples of other work that the band brings with them and ask what they like about these recordings. They may like the vocal sound on one song, the drums on another. Take these ideas with you as you begin the recording and mixing process, and help them to find a good sound they're happy with.

Deciding how long a session you need to finish a project can vary depending on a lot of factors, and it's usually up to you as the engineer to decide how much time will be needed for any given project. Typically an eight-hour session is good for tracking the basics of one song—if the band is well polished. Factor in another four- to five-hour session for overdubs, if necessary and they almost always are. Remember, overdubbing is where you either add additional audio (or replace bad audio) in your session, a process generally done during the mixing stages of a production. In general, try to limit your sessions to no more than the aforementioned eight hours per day; performing music is a surprisingly physically demanding job, and you'll find that your clients waste a lot less time if they're well rested, both physically and mentally.

Once recording day comes, every engineer has a different way of dealing with things; most, myself included, start by tracking, in a multitrack environment, rhythm section (drums and bass) together with a click track and scratch rhythm guitar and scratch vocal (*scratch* meaning "on the fly, for temporary reference purposes"), followed by rhythm guitar, lead guitar, and finally vocals. From there, you might find a lot of other things you can add here or there—extra percussion, vocals overdubs, instrument layers.

Despite most bands' enthusiasm to finish up the project, I always schedule my first mixing session at least a week after tracking ends. By this time, the band has enough time to rest, relax their ears, and get ready to listen objectively to the near-finished product. Their input at this stage will be very valuable, so make sure they're in the best condition to offer their advice. I usually do mixing sessions in a one-song-a-day format, where we make a good attempt to finish a single song mix in an eight-hour session. This usually works well, if the client has the budget to dedicate to mixing in this way. Sometimes, a client won't have the budget to spend doing full-day mix sessions, in which case quick mixes are done, up to twelve in one day, and then the band selects a few songs to spend more time on, if they can.

After the final mixes are decided upon, have one last listening session a week later and declare the product finished.

Sample Studio Checklist

When starting a new project, I typically create a sample checklist with the help of the band, prioritizing elements that we feel are very important. I try to start from the smallest element up—and build the recording piece by piece. The checklist is also extremely helpful as a visual aid to help keep you on task throughout the production process. The following is an actual sample checklist that I used with one of my clients. It should give you some insight into what the process was like.

Next Sunday
North Meets South
Studio Checklist
1. "North Meets South"

—Track scratch guitar
—Track scratch vocal
—Double guitar track
—Overdub vocal
—Percussion
—Mixing

[Track] 2. "Oh My Life"
—Track scratch guitar
—Track scratch vocal

—Track drums with scratch bass

—Retrack guitar #1

—Retrack guitar #2

—Track bass

—Overdub vocals

—Dub chorus vocals

—Track keys

—Mixing

3. "Places"

—Track scratch guitar

—Track scratch vocals

—Track drums

—Track electric guitar

—Track electric guitar double

—Track acoustic guitar #1

—Track acoustic guitar #2

—Track bass

—Track vocals

—Track vocal overdub

—Track chorus

—Track keys

—Mixing

4. "Sunrise"

—Track acoustic guitar #1

—Track drums

—Track bass

—Mixing

[Date] _____ _____

[Album Name] _____

Studio Checklist

[Track 1 Name] _____

_____

_____

_____

[Track 2 Name] _____

_____

_____

_____

[Track 3 Name] _____

_____

_____

_____

[Track 4 Name] _____

_____

_____

_____

[Track 5 Name] _____

_____

_____

_____

Time Frame

As you may have already found out the hard way, establishing a career in a business as fickle as the recording industry can take time. Starting your own business is one of the few fast-track options to establishing a career in your chosen field, but don't be discouraged when you realize how long it may actually take to get a good client base, produce quality products, and become self-sustainable. That's a more eloquent way of saying "don't quit your day job"—at least at first. In many cases it can take years to build a good client base and begin turning a profit.

When deciding to open your own studio, think about the local economy. First, how strong is your local music scene? How big of a demand is there for your services? And, most importantly, can your skills compete with the big guys in the local recording business? If there're only a few bands doing anything notable in town and few others giving their dreams of rock stardom a shot, you may not have enough local business possibilities to sustain yourself. Even with the best equipment and a great set of skills, if there's no demand, you won't do well enough to keep the doors open just recording small demos and radio spots.

The other thing to realize is that money goes fast. In chapter 5 we'll talk more in detail about the financial planning that it takes to start and maintain a business. You need to manage your finances carefully in order to make sure you have working capital to make your business last. Starting a business is a lot more than buying equipment—you'll need to pay your taxes and business licensing fees, and keep enough money in the bank to live off of while your business takes off. I know it seems really difficult, but if you pay careful attention to your financial management skills, you'll be fine.

For most businesses, it takes a while to get your name out there to those who need you, and that's especially true in a business like the music industry, which relies on close-knit personal connections. Don't be discouraged; until clients are ready to trust you, you might find business slow. Do your best to network and build up a good reputation. The rest will hopefully fall into place.

Know Your Competition

Before you open your studio to paying customers, take some time to research and know the competition.

In many locales, unless you're in a major city and have a wealth of clients to pick from, there may already be too much competition for you to remain viable unless you're confident you can offer a phenomenal product at a better value than the other local businesses in the same game. I've personally seen many operations fold simply because there wasn't enough business to go around. Understanding what your competition does and how they do it can help you greatly.

Research your competition. One of the best scenarios you can possibly have is a major player who produces an inferior product but retains a majority of the market share because they're the only game in town. Ask around. How have past experiences with competition in the area been? Identify your competition's weaknesses. Do you have better faith in your abilities and can you offer a superior product? Great. Can you offer a better product at a more attractive price? Excellent. Obviously, getting clients to trust you over the long-established competition will be hard, but many businesses have been in your shoes and have succeeded just fine.

When you decide to research your competition, there are a few key areas that you should focus on. Let's take a look at how you can best figure out what you need to do in order to remain competitive (and stay in business in the process):

- **Equipment.** How does your equipment compare? If your main competitor is using a Pro Tools HD system with Apogee converters and Neve microphone preamps, your Digidesign 003-K with a set of Behringer microphone preamps can't really compare. If your microphone selection doesn't include industry standards that most projects require, you can't command a higher rate. To stay on top of what the other pros in your field are doing, check out some magazines such as *EQ* and *Tape Op*.
- **Recording space.** How is your competitor's space compared to yours? Do you have good-sounding live rooms and dead-sounding isolation rooms? If the answer is no, then you can't compete with a studio that does.
- **Software.** Are you running Pro Tools and Logic, or some other smaller, proprietary software package? If you aren't compatible with projects done in most larger commercial studios, you don't have much chance to charge a high rate. It's especially important if you want to bring in major clients, because they'll demand cross-studio compatibility—something these major software packages ensure, if nothing else.
- **Last but not least, your skill level.** We'll talk about this more later, but if your skills aren't on par with the best engineer at your main competitor, then chances are you're not going to be able to command a similar rate.

Here's a project for you to try. Using this questionnaire, find out some information about your local competitors. Make as many copies as you need, and it'll not only let you see what kind of standards you'll need to maintain, but it'll allow you to average your competition's numbers against yours—and get a good idea of their financial picture.

Studio Name: _____

_____

Location: _____

_____

Recording Spaces: _____

_____

Square Feet: _____

_____

Interface: _____

_____

Preamps: _____

_____

Pro Tools Compatible?: _____

_____

Price Per Hour, Tracking Space: _____

_____

Price Per Hour, Engineer: _____

_____

Hourly Minimums?: _____

_____

Microphone Selection: _____

_____

Clients will judge your overall worth on what your skills can do for them; if you can't do the same editing and mixing magic that the big guys can, you're not going to be able to compete.

As you can see, it's a very competitive business. It pays, literally and figuratively, to pursue going above and beyond—even if the initial investment for doing so is higher than you expected. There's nothing wrong with setting your sights a little on the higher side, especially if there's little competition in your area.

03 Writing a Business Plan

Being unprepared is one of the worst things you can do for yourself as a small business owner. The little details—even broad questions you feel you've already answered, including "What does my business do?"—are extremely important.

Writing a business plan is a complicated affair, but it's something that you'll need to do—especially if you want to procure financing for your studio. Many times, business plans aren't referenced by anybody but the business owner. That fact doesn't make it any less important; it's still a vital document, even if nobody else is going to see it. Writing out a business plan gives you that black-and-white roadmap to getting your business off the ground. Still, a business plan is even more important to those you go to hat-in-hand looking for a loan. Business plans are a sign that you've "got it together," so to speak.

As we will discuss later on, financing is getting increasingly hard to acquire in today's economy. Since I started my business in fall 2003, there's been a major shift in how business financing works. I remember obtaining business credit with a little work and my personal guarantee that my new start-up was worthy of the financial backing; now, it's a very hard competition for every available dollar, because many banks simply can't afford the frequent losses that today's economy produces among small businesses. A good, solid business plan is absolutely necessary to get anywhere in this process. It's also necessary if you're looking to take on private investors at any time in the near future.

So, I've convinced you to write a business plan, you say? Good! Let's take the bull by the horns. This isn't the easiest thing to do, but once you do, you'll be so happy—especially the first time you need some direction and find the way out of a potentially sticky situation by following your business plan!

In simple terms, a business plan is a document in which you as a new business owner set your goals and plan out how to make the business sustainable. You'll detail every step of the process—how you plan to raise financing, how you will market and develop your studio and its products, and how you'll make money in the long run. It's generally considered a confidential document, open only to the principal executives at a business and the business's potential financial lenders. This isn't a document for public consumption. You, as the business owner, will be in charge of marketing your business to the public. Think of your business plan as your marketing effort to lenders and investors and, most importantly, as your roadmap to success.

Of course, a business plan is very important for the long-term growth of your business, too. It's your goals on paper—and how you hope to achieve them. Referencing this business plan will become extremely valuable for you personally in the future. While even the most elaborate business plan can't guarantee success, think of it as a plan of action for utilizing your business's assets to the fullest potential and a document to keep you grounded as your successes grow.

The Elements of a Business Plan

So what goes into a good business plan? It's a lot easier than you might think, but it requires a certain familiarity with your business, and the patience to explain things to nontechnical individuals. You should give potential investors a good idea of who you are, what your background is, and what you wish to accomplish with your business. It shouldn't be too long, but it should be as comprehensive as possible.

Also, you'll mention what you're going to do to make money. This is where you'll describe, in great detail, what day-to-day operations in your business will be. You'll need to tell potential investors how your recording process works, what makes your studio unique, and why you're worth risking their money on.

Financial planning is another important part of any business plan. You should be able to talk, in detail, about the financial realities of your business. You need to show that you've got a viable chance at being able to pay back any loans made to you on your business's behalf, and you should be able to provide supporting evidence that backs up this assertion. This is one of the most important sections of any business plan; you may think that your recording studio is bulletproof, but being able to show how you'll be working toward becoming financially successful is highly recommended.

Now that we've talked about the basics of a business plan, let's take a look at the individual elements you'll need to include. For the purposes of this example, I'll focus on five key elements of a successful business plan:

- Executive Summary
- Business Summary
- Business Description
- Market Analysis
- Break-Even Point

Executive Summary

Audio engineering and producing music in general is a complicated endeavor. It's a complex vocation and no matter how easy modern products make it look, there's a great deal of skill involved. It's hard to explain what we engineers do—how many of your relatives still don't understand what you do for a living (and let's not forget the occasional relative who asks, "When are you getting a real job?")?

A large chunk of your business plan will be explaining to your potential lenders what you do. It's a lot more than just saying "recording studio." Fortunately, since you know your business better than anybody, this can be easy to do—with a little bit of organization.

The first part of any good business plan is your executive summary. Basically, an executive summary acts as the preamble to your business plan. It's a multipart section that talks about the basics of how your business has the potential to be successful.

1. You'll introduce the business and explain what your business objectives and goals will be. This gives your reader insight into what exactly your business does. They'll be able to get a good idea what type of business they're looking at just by reading your objectives. This is where you'll also make mention of your target market, how fast you plan to expand, and anything else a potential lender needs to know.

2. You will list specific objectives for the business plan itself. Whether you intend to use this plan to obtain outside lenders, entice investors, or simply to better guide your business, here's where you let the reader know what purpose the information you've compiled has.

3. It's a good idea to list what's called "keys to success." What does your business offer that the competition doesn't? Where do you see a need for your

niche services? If your customer service will be the best in town, this is where you can brag about it.

Business Summary

The next piece of the business plan puzzle is called the "Business Summary." Here's where you'll go into more specifics about the start-up phase of your business. You'll define how you plan to get the ball rolling and what type of structure your business will have.

Writing a good business summary is actually quite different than an executive summary. An executive summary is a condensed version of what your business does; a few short paragraphs that introduce you and what you're planning to do. The business summary will go into the gritty details of the costs and processes behind actually opening the studio doors.

A good business summary also offers information about where the business will be located— in your case, out of your home—and information about how the legal structure will be formed. It's also a good place to lay out your start-up costs and projected expenses within the first year of running your business.

In writing the business summary, ask yourself some important questions:

- How will your start-up be structured? Talk about the legal structure of your business and where you plan to run the business.
- How will you pay for start-up costs?
- What steps need to be taken before you open the doors to paying clients? Discuss matters of financial importance, such as renovation, acoustic treatment, equipment selection, and legal matters that must be taken care of first.

Business Description

While it may seem redundant to call the next section "business description," this is where you really dig in to describe what you do. Having day-to-day operations separated into this distinct section gives you the space to really brag about your business's strong offerings without forcing it on someone who doesn't have the time to read it. Many lenders will want to know just the basics—what your assets and liabilities are, what your business's potential is, and how you plan to pull it off. But some potential partners will take an interest in your day-to-day operations and will want to know in greater detail what it is that you do. Explaining this to someone who isn't so familiar with the ins and outs of recording can be difficult, so you'll want to take your time and do it right.

Aside from a general description of what you're planning to offer the world, you'll want to go into detail about each individual service your studio will perform. If you're providing mastering and other value-added services, here's where you would describe them.

Writing a business description is probably the easiest part of the whole business plan. You'll basically be talking about the things you know best—running a recording studio. But you'll also need to give insight into some more in-depth items, too, to give yourself and potential lenders an idea of the big picture.

Ask yourself:

- What does your recording studio plan to offer your clients, and how do you explain that to a nontechnical individual?
- What can your studio offer that others in your market area do not? Give specific examples and be as detailed as possible.
- What would you want an outsider to know about your recording studio? If there's anything you feel a potential lender should know about the way your business runs—from how a client session is handled, to how you market your services—you should be able to explain it clearly.

Market Analysis

This is the section that will require the most research on your part. Simply put, this is the section that lays out who your competition is, who will want to buy your services, and the trends associated with your business. It may not be something you've thought about until now, but it's important to include if you're trying to get someone interested in investing in your business

Doing a market analysis for yourself is a great idea, too. Every year you can take stock of your competition and see who expands, who goes out of business, or who moves to a smaller facility. By monitoring this information year after year, you'll be able to follow (and eventually foresee) trends in your local scene, and it will allow you to maintain a reference for eventual upgrades. Being able to strike when the iron is hottest always results in better market positioning.

In analyzing your target market, ask yourself some important questions:

- Who is your target clientele?
- How often do they spend money on these services?
- What's the average project cost for a client?
- What are major trends in the business that you need to stay abreast of?

The market analysis is basically your way of explaining who will make your business successful (other than you, of course). Making sure you know who you're after allows you to precisely plan your future marketing strategies to maximize the impact and visibility you have with your potential clients.

Break-Even Point

Another good element of any good business plan—and one that will become your most dynamic element yet—is called the break-even point. The break-even point is where all of your business debts are met by a certain amount of revenue.

In order to show your break-even point you'll need to show several variables in writing. First is the amount of profit you need to make to cover your monthly bills. For example, your business's monthly expenses could be $1,250. This might cover a $700 rent payment, $300 in loans, and $250 in monthly utilities (a broad category that breaks down to include "accessory costs," everything from Internet to additional electricity needed for studio operations). Second, you'll need to show how many billable hours—or whatever unit you choose to bill your clients—it will take to reach that goal. You'll also need to keep in mind when your clients can pay—and if you're going to be able to make your numbers with the outstanding invoices you have. This is why many recording studios require payment up front for services rendered. If you choose to bill your clients, be prepared for the fact that some clients will default, and others will take a long time to pay. How long you're willing to wait for them to pay is up to you, but I suggest asking for payment within fourteen days, if you choose not to go the prepaid route.

Knowing that you will spend $1,250 well before your first client comes in, you now have the necessary information to properly plan a goal to work toward. Including your 13.3% self-employment tax, if your hourly rate is $35, you can easily figure that you need to bill and receive payment for just under 41 hours of studio time a month to meet your break-even point. After also paying taxes, any money you make from your break-even point onward is pure profit, which can be used any way you allocate. Of course, part of that may be your salary for running the business—or not, if your business is too new to afford the luxury of a paycheck for the owner.

To summarize, finding your break-even point is quite easy:

- What are your monthly costs for running the business? Include rent, utilities, taxes, and any loan payments you need to make.
- What is your hourly billable rate? Do you prefer flat-rate or hourly pricing, and which one offers you the best advantage?
- How many billable hours will you need to invoice (and be paid for) to make your monthly costs?

Sample Business Plan

Making a business plan might sound hard, but if you've got a good enough grasp on this industry to open your own recording studio business, it'll be a breeze explaining the important things. You don't have to get too wordy; if your business plan lands on someone else's desk for review, chances are they'll appreciate a concise, clear, and condensed version of the facts.

Here's a sample business plan that you can reference. Remember, just as with selecting microphones for recording, one size does not fit all. The following example shows the general elements that should be included for this type of business, but you'll need to heavily modify this document for your own personal needs.

John Smith Studios

EXECUTIVE SUMMARY

The purpose of this business plan is to offer a roadmap to the successful operation of John Smith Studios, a proposed recording studio facility and audio production service located in the San Francisco Bay area. John Smith Studios will tentatively begin operations on January 10, 2011. John Smith is an accomplished audio engineer and music producer, previously working with many clients as a freelance engineer. Mr. Smith hopes to leverage this experience and industry contacts to the benefit of his new business.

What follows is a brief summary of the information contained within this business plan, as applies to John Smith Studios.

1. John Smith Studios plans to open for public business on January 10, 2011.
2. The sole purpose of John Smith Studios will be to offer affordable, high-quality audio production services to the business's target market, as discussed in the market analysis segment of this business plan.
3. Initially, the business will offer recording services to solo artists and vocalists, clients who do not require much recording space. As the business evolves and profit can support the addition of additional recording facilities, more clients with larger projects can be accommodated.
4. The business also plans to distinguish itself from existing competition by use of high-quality equipment unlike anything utilized at this time. Clients can expect technological innovations to be a forefront focus of the business, allowing better quality and more efficient production.

John Smith Studios, and proprietor John Smith, are tremendously confident in the business's ability to attract and retain a quality paying customer base. This plan intends to serve as a one-stop guide to all activities leading up to and within the everyday operations of the business and will allow management of the business to have a firm hold on the direction the business must take in order to remain profitable for not only itself, but also for the lenders and partners who trust their names to the project.

BUSINESS SUMMARY

John Smith Studios will open in January 2011 with John Smith as the sole proprietor of record. This business will be run solely by John Smith, and will be legally structured as a sole proprietorship.

John Smith is currently the sole financial investor of the project and anticipates investing $24,000 of his own money into the business. This $24,000 is currently in an interest-bearing savings account, and is considered "cash on hand." Aside from this initial self-invested seed money, John Smith estimates that he will need an additional $20,000 for equipment and business expenses. Mr. Smith plans to acquire this through partnering with low-interest business lenders.

John Smith Studios will be established as an at-home business, utilizing a newly refurbished space in John Smith's garage. Many home recording studios have been commercially successful; John Smith Studios hopes to follow this trend. This will cut down on the overhead of the business, as it will be included in the monthly mortgage payment that John Smith is already paying. This monthly mortgage expense will become a burden of the business, for the purposes of maintaining a quality location to operate from without incurring additional undue expenses.

John Smith Studios plans to utilize exceptionally advanced recording equipment to manage both a high-quality end product and an exceedingly satisfactory client experience. Equipment purchasing encompasses the bulk of start-up spending for most recording studio start-ups. This studio is no exception.

- Approximately $39,000 will be used for equipment purchases. This is to include an Avid Pro Tools HD core system and Control 24 mixing console, both sizable purchases. The remaining budget will be spent purchasing other vital equipment including microphones, cabling, and accessories.

- $2,000 will be earmarked for modifications to the home's garage. As this room was sold partially finished, refurbishing costs will be minimal. A $2,000 investment would cover isolation room construction, furniture for studio equipment and clients, and acoustic paneling treatment. This investment can be broken down as follows:

  - $450 for acoustic paneling and diffusers to help isolate and shape the recording control room's acoustics.
  - $500 for acoustic paneling and construction materials for an isolation room; this room will be 5 feet by 5 feet by 8 feet tall and will create a small "room within a room" for the purpose of isolating recording vocalists and soloists from the recording work area, known as the control room.
  - $500 will be used for labor (in building the isolation room and finishing the control room).
  - $550 will be earmarked for furniture. This will include office chairs, a pair of couches (for clients to use when working), indirect lighting, and desks for audio equipment.

- Another $2,000 will operate as an emergency fund. This is money the business owner plans to keep in an interest-bearing savings account for the duration of the life of the $20,000 loan. This will be used as emergency cash for equipment repairs or issues that may arise. If this money remains untouched to the end of the loan—and the business continues operating in a positive cash-flow environment—the $2,000 will act as the final payment on the loan. This ensures that the business will remain free of debilitating revolving debt in case of hard times.

- $1,000 will be used strictly for marketing purposes within the first six months of operation. While this number is low by industry standards, it reflects a focused campaign aimed at advertising in pre-picked locations for maximum exposure to the target market and with more positive impressions than anywhere else. This money is earmarked as follows:

  - $500 to establish an Internet presence, including the creation of a small website, business card and logo design, and online portfolio design
  - $100 for six-months' worth of hosting fees, paid on a biannual basis
  - $400 to be used for sponsorships, pay-as-you-go Internet advertising, paid print and classified ads.

After the initial six-month advertising campaign, the studio will budget between $150 and $200 monthly to continue advertising via the most effective campaigns.

Day-to-day operations at John Smith Studios will consist of hourly sessions, where clients may utilize the equipment and recording knowledge of the studio to produce audio recordings, which can be either musical or nonmusical in nature. John Smith Studios strives to use the latest techniques and most high-tech equipment to make the best recordings in the market.

These recordings will mainly be used by musicians as promotional tools, allowing them to also sell the songs for a profit. John Smith Studios plans to make a profit primarily by selling recording time by the hour; however, some clients will be negotiated "day rates" and "song rates," allowing projects a small discount if a block of time is paid in full.

By 2013, John Smith Studios plans to offer a mastering service, taking music projects one final step in the completion of the recording. The mastering engineer will sonically polish songs to sound their best on a variety of playback systems, cleaning up the editing in the track and producing a final radio—or sales-ready—masterpiece.

Clearly, John Smith and John Smith Studios feel properly positioned to be a top resource for the growing professional entertainer and pro audio market in San Francisco.

MARKET ANALYSIS

The target market for John Smith Studios is the musician's market. The average person the business hopes to attract as a customer is a musician, age twenty-one through forty-five, who's interested in recording in the facility, either as a solo performer or as part of a band. This market will make up the vast majority of sales for the business. Another smaller but equally important segment is the corporate market. These customers will require smaller-scale projects, including music beds (the "on hold" music you hear on the telephone and music you hear in commercials), announcements, telephone menu messages, and Internet-ready podcasts for employees or investors. While this area is smaller than the musician's market, John Smith Studios expects this type of work—which takes very little effort or overhead to perform—will help, especially in slow months of the year (typically the holidays and summer, when most bands are on tour).

Competition is found in the four other studios located within 25 miles of John Smith Studios' location. These four studios offer varying degrees of quality, with only one comparable to the projected quality of John Smith Studios, with equipment variety, equipment quality, and technical skill being the primary strengths of John Smith Studios.

These competitor studios charge between $20 and $55 per hour for their services. John Smith Studios will set its initial studio price at $35 per hour, with the option to charge corporate clients a set rate for their requested work. This hourly fee will include recording and mixing services.

Understanding the market and how to meet its needs will be one of the cornerstones of John Smith Studios. As such, John Smith Studios will spend an initial budget of $1,000 on marketing, which will include sponsorship of local musician's events, placement of advertisements in local fringe publications, and local music blogs. This will allow a direct connection to the artists, and in turn will help keep the business continually educated on trends within the local musician's scene.

In summary:

- John Smith Studios' primary target market is working musicians with a need for recorded music for promotional and sale purposes.

- The target market is primarily male, ages twenty-one through forty-five.

- Most projects produced by the studio will be full-band recordings; however, to maximize profit potential while setting up the full recording space, John Smith Studios will begin by recording soloists, vocalists, and hip-hop artists, which requires much less space.

- The average hourly rate for John Smith Studios will be $35.

- The secondary market for John Smith Studios will be corporate clients who will primarily use John Smith Studios for production of advertising audio.

BREAK-EVEN ESTIMATES

The business will start operations with a deficit of $1,250 per month. This includes the cost of rent ($700), the projected loan payment of $300 (a $20,000 loan at a reasonable percentage rate), and $250 earmarked for business expenses, including additional utilities and supplies such as paper, ink, replacement parts, and servicing.

- Monthly Deficit: $1,250

- Monthly Break-Even Point: $1,250

- Monthly Break-Even Billable Hours: 36

- Hourly rate, average client: $35

- Daily profit, assuming all eight hours in one work day billed: $280

- Maximum potential weekly profit, assuming no overtime or additional services, and five billable days worked per week: $1,400

CONCLUSION

John Smith Studios is ready to establish itself as a market leader in the San Francisco recording studio market. By offering superior quality equipment and knowledge, John Smith plans to offer a value-priced product with a very high quality output.

This combination of fair pricing (brought on by the economical choice of a home studio location) and expert knowledge will create a business with large potential profit per month. In fact, one week's profit could potentially reach $1,400—assuming all billable hours in one week are reserved by clients.

With a relatively low debt and very few expenses, John Smith Studios will be able to easily turn a profit, if business can be grown at a steady pace. While recording studios are plentiful in the area, none offer the amenities and quality service that only John Smith Studios will offer. With a commitment to being the best recording provider in the Bay area, John Smith Studios has the potential to become a major player—and thus expand greatly in both clientele and studio quality.

Getting Started

With your business plan in hand, it's time to get started. You know where you're going, you have a good idea how you're going to get there, and you also know how you'll pay for it.

While I'm assuming you're a great audio engineer and ready for the challenge of producing great music for paying customers in your home studio, this is where we start the really hard part. Setting up your chosen equipment and hitting record is one thing—and it's by far the easiest part of running a business like this. Over the next couple of chapters, we're going to talk about the business end of a recording studio business. It's really important stuff that you shouldn't overlook. I promise we'll get back to the fun stuff soon enough.

First Things First

We've talked about evaluating your skills for running an actual recording studio—and hopefully you've found yourself technically proficient and up to the challenge. We're going to leave behind the audio engineering stuff for a little bit, because we've got some business to take care of.

First, have you chosen a name for your business yet? You'll be required to register your business with the local and state entities that regulate business in your area, and that requires being unique—and, potentially, a few bucks to spare. Registering this name can cost you anywhere between $10 and $100, depending on your municipality's requirements. In my home state of Missouri, you can register a "fictitious name" registration for $7.95. Your fees may be higher, but it's something you certainly need. Be sure to factor this into your initial start-up costs. You'll use this name on your advertising materials, which include your social networking sites. That being said, you may consider using your name as part of your business's name. While a recording studio is rarely a brand name itself (think Abbey Road Studios, a real-life studio that's spawned numerous hardware and software products), marketing yourself and your top-notch engineering skills as a commodity can really help, especially if your skills offer something exceptional.

How do you know if the name you've chosen is already in use? This is something you'll need to take up with your local regulatory authority—most times, you'll be able to search online. In my home state of Missouri, it's very easy to search for businesses through the Secretary of State's website, but some states are very different and require you to phone or write for this information.

Banking and Credit

In the next chapter, we'll talk more in-depth about the complex financial situations that come from running your own business, especially when it comes to financing your opening. Getting financing is really hard in today's turbulent economy; even in the last few years that I've been in business, the game has changed considerably. In order to fully tackle the things we talk about in chapter 5, you'll need to establish a business checking account. At this stage it's also possible to start looking into establishing credit relationships—or *trade lines*—with other businesses. This can help you immensely later on, as long as you keep your credit in great shape.

Establishing a business checking account at a local bank is generally an easy process. You'll need to be a legally formed business first, something which you'll learn about in more detail in the next chapter. As a small business, you'll be able to get some excellent offers; small businesses are a valued customer at most banks offering business checking. Because of the sensitive nature of their establishing charters, some credit unions—even if you bank there currently—cannot accept business accounts, so your best bet will be to work closely with an established commercial bank.

While many business checking accounts can be opened easily online, it's usually better to meet in-person with a banking representative at your local branch. The rep can explain in finer detail the nuances of the different account types and work with you to establish a banking relationship that best suits your needs. You'll need to bring a business license or other proof of being a legitimate business, and you'll also have to supply your own personal information. Under some situations, they may require you to be a personal guarantor on the account, especially as a new start-up business. Don't worry, this is only in case you overdraw your account and require the bank to cover it—which should be avoided at all costs.

Once you've established a business checking account that works for you, it's time to start looking into business credit. This is different than what we'll tackle in chapter 5; this is establishing small-dollar credit accounts for items you might need in daily operation. It's best to start this process early and work hard to build up a great credit profile.

Business credit has changed a great deal in the last few years. When I first started my business in 2003 the world financial market hadn't collapsed upon itself just yet. Business credit for legitimate businesses was relatively easy to come by. I remember within the first year I had several credit accounts with great merchants and I was able to get short-term credit for just about any basic supply I needed—from printer ink to shipping services—all in the name of the business. Unfortunately the times have changed drastically. Business credit is no longer the easy-to-access resource it once was, in part due to people setting up false businesses to circumvent poor personal credit.

That being said, building business credit can be done if handled responsibly. The first thing to evaluate is your personal credit. Knowing where you stand will help you immensely because better terms and much quicker financing are available to those with great personal credit scores, even if the credit is solely for your business. Just like starting a bank account, you'll be asked to be the personal guarantor for your business's credit—where the lender uses your personal credit score in lieu of your business's credit. Most lenders ask for a personal guarantor because your business lacks sufficient credit on its own, and the lenders can't establish an account without a baseline rating on how likely you are to pay your bills on time.

To start building business credit solely on the merit of your business, you'll need to do a few things right.

1. **Register a telephone number for your business.** While this may seem redundant in our world of cell phones, an inexpensive business landline—verifiable via 411 directory assistance services—is very important for being a legitimate business in the eyes of most lenders. After obtaining your number, which can cost as little as $15 per month in some markets, make your number visible to directory assistance nationwide by registering with websites such as ListYourself (www.listyourself.net). If you don't want to get a landline, some services—such as MagicJack, which offers Internet-based phone service through your computer—will work; services such as Google

Voice generally do not. Sure, it's old-fashioned, but most business lenders view a landline as proof of a legitimate business.

2. **Open an account with Dun & Bradstreet.** D&B, and their proprietary Paydex scoring system, is the primary source that many business lenders go to in order to determine your business credit, the other two being Experian and Equifax Business. Establishing your business file with D&B is easy and doesn't cost you anything. Contrary to what D&B's trained salespeople will tell you, obtaining a Paydex score and D&B file for your business does not require any purchases to be made through the company (the most common pitch is a Credit Builder package that will cost you several hundred dollars). Call D&B at 1-866-705-5711 and request a D&B number be assigned to your business. This is especially important at this stage in the game because you, as a multipurpose recording facility, may need to bid on government contracts. It takes a couple of months for your file to start showing any activity, but they should be able to give you your credit file number immediately. Use this when filling out applications for business credit, when asked. Many lenders will pull your D&B file when you apply, regardless if you provide your number or not.

3. **Establish small credit accounts.** In order to build your D&B Paydex credit score, establish small accounts with vendors that offer thirty- or sixty-day credit terms. At the time of this writing, companies such as Uline (www.uline.com), Reliable (www.reliable.com), and Quill (www.quill.com) were standard go-to choices for new businesses. Order from these businesses with your new account and pay very promptly—they tend to report to your D&B file very quickly.

4. **Follow your progress.** Call D&B and register for their eUpdate program. You'll be able to monitor your D&B file frequently (they generally make changes on Saturday nights). Once you see yourself with a Paydex score of 80 or higher, you're in good shape. Give it some time, though—until you have a full five trade lines showing, even with a Paydex score of 80 you're unlikely to get approved for much.

After you've followed these steps, you'll start building credit for your business. Give it a few months, or even a year—and you'll find that your business will be able to stand on its own when applying for credit, without your personal guarantee needed. Sure, it's a time-consuming, patience-stretching process, but it'll be worth it in the long run.

Contracts

Before you take your first paying client, you need to start thinking about what kind of contract you'll have with your customers. Contracts may seem like an unnecessary formality (especially in a socially driven business such as music), but I promise you: The first time you get burned without a contract in place, you'll wish you could turn back the clock and make a contract a mandatory part of your recording process. It can cost you thousands.

In the summer of 2004, I took on some clients who were rising stars in the local scene. They had used another local studio and were very unhappy with the quality they received in the finished product, so they needed their studio sessions finished. I offered to work with them to produce the project, remixing the raw sessions to their satisfaction and using my studio to record additional overdubs. I would also be mastering the project and producing a radio-ready EP. We made a verbal, handshake-sealed contract that I would perform the work and that I would be paid a continued percentage of their gig earnings until the total was paid off, close to $2,000. As part of my contract, I would also mix their live gigs, and provide live recording services for one large upcoming gig. I thought I was working with good people whose word was worth everything.

Unfortunately, they defaulted. They defaulted big time. I didn't make one dime out of this project, even after putting in a lot of my own time and more energy than I care to remember—not to mention the billable hours that could've been billed to someone who actually paid.

If I had had a contract with these particular clients, things might have ended up much differently.

Contracts do two things: One, they limit your risk and liabilities. That's a fancy way of saying that these contracts will help keep your business out of the crosshairs of a lawsuit, and they'll help limit how much money you could potentially lose on deadbeat clients. It's a legal agreement between you and your client, and the terms of your business dealings are spelled out in black-and-white. Second, it aligns expectations on both sides of the table. You're able to spell out the terms of doing business and make sure that your clients know everything that will be performed for them and when it will be done. Second, it'll spell out the financial details and every other aspect of your temporary partnership with your client.

Having worked in the music business for over ten years, I can tell you one thing: Musicians don't like contracts. They're not contract-type people. Most deals in the music business are very informal until you get to indie-label status or above. Unfortunately for you, being formal and businesslike can scare off some potential clients who'd prefer to do things "under the table." But don't be discouraged: These types of clients aren't worth having, as they'll tend to lowball your estimates, fail to pay on time, and change the terms of your business relationship as the process goes forward. Don't worry about losing these clients—I know it always hurts to lose potential money, but keep in mind that the best clients will always pay you on time and will have no problem signing a contract. Those who choose not to conduct themselves professionally aren't worth your time.

Take a look at the boilerplate contract that I use with most of my clients. You're welcome to use it. While the wording may not always work for every situation, this is where I start. As always, you should consult with a good lawyer before using a standard contract; the laws differ in every state and you might need to fine-tune your wording to be compliant. Don't get caught on a technicality because you didn't make sure the law was on your side!

Sample Band Recording Contract

Here's an actual contract that I frequently use in my studio business—the names have been changed, but everything else is exactly how my client signed the agreement. I've used this same boilerplate agreement several times, with much success.

One disclaimer: This contract was prepared with the help of my attorney to comply with State of Missouri laws and regulations. Things may need to be worded differently for use in your business; if you do choose to use this boilerplate contract, please verify with a trusted attorney that the terms and conditions stated in this contract fall within legal guidelines of your state and municipality. An illegal contract is just as bad (if not worse) than no contract at all!

Introduction.

A. This contract serves as the final and legally binding agreement between John Smith, a St. Louis, Missouri–based music producer and audio engineer, d/b/a John Smith Sound, a sole proprietorship recording studio registered in St. Louis County, Missouri (hereby referred to as "PRODUCER"), and *[SAMPLE BAND]*, a musical group, and their representative of record, JANE DOE (hereby referred to as "ARTIST"). ARTIST and PRODUCER agree to the terms within this contract as a finally binding agreement.

Section 1: Production and Delivery.

A. This contract serves as the written legal documentation of expectations for both parties.

B. PRODUCER agrees to the production, recording, and delivery of a fully recorded, mixed, and mastered album not to exceed 12 songs.

C. ARTIST agrees to a two-month preproduction period to start at the date of signing this contract and ending on the first day of actual studio recording. During this preproduction period, it will be understood that both ARTIST and PRODUCER will work together to lay out the framework for the recording studio process as well as the creative direction of the album.

D. ARTIST agrees to supply PRODUCER with demo/rough mix versions of all anticipated songs, if they exist, within 30 days of the signing of this contract.

E. ARTIST agrees that in the event the album's length as agreed upon exceeds 12 songs, a flat rate of $250 per additional song, payable in advance, will be paid for recording time and resources incurred in this additional action.

Section 2: Costs and Terms.

A. ARTIST agrees to a predetermined fee of $1,800 for the start-to-finish term of the project. This cost includes applicable studio time, mixing, mastering, and pre-production.

B. DEPOSIT. Artist agrees to a nonrefundable deposit of one-third the total cost, $600, payable in advance, applicable to the total overall cost of the recording process.

C. PRODUCER agrees to no points or splits on album sales.

Traditionally, music producers are paid in "points," or percentage points on the sales of an album. It's becoming rarer to get high-point deals, but there's still money to be made. As an independent producer, you may want to avoid relying on points—the truth is, many albums don't do very well at all. Always receive at least enough cash up front to cover your operating expenses of the project, and to cover your personal overhead.

Section 3: Crediting.

A. ARTIST agrees to credit PRODUCER in the following manner within the album credits on all formats:

a. "Produced by John Smith & *[SAMPLE BAND]*"

b. "Engineer: John Smith"

c. "Second Engineer: TBA"

Please note: many interns and second engineers frequently work on studio sessions with PRODUCER. This section is to allow them a proper credit for their work if necessary.

Section 4: Added Services.

A. PRODUCER agrees, to the best of his ability, to provide consulting services to ARTIST, including, but not limited to: digital distribution, submission to radio outlets and A&R opportunities, tour & production consulting, and any other relevant opportunities to insure the success of the album.

Section 5: Force Majeure.

A. PRODUCER agrees to deliver a finished product in a timely manner, as is expected, unless circumstances beyond the control of either PRODUCER or ARTIST and their representatives occur. In such a situation where delivery of a final product is either delayed or impossible due to mechanical failure of recording equipment, communication failure, illness, injury, recording media failure, acts of nature, theft, or any unforeseen circumstance, ARTIST agrees to pursue no relief other than a mutually agreeable time to begin recording lost material at no additional expense to ARTIST.

Section 6: Confidentiality and Arbitration.

A. PRODUCER agrees to closely guard all rough mixes, demo mixes, alternate mixes, and unmastered tracks to avoid any commercial loss on behalf of ARTIST. ARTIST agrees to not release any rough mixes, demo mixes (recorded with PRODUCER), and unmastered tracks in any format.

B. ARTIST agrees to keep all proprietary knowledge of studio operations—including proprietary techniques utilized on behalf of this project by PRODUCER—confidential.

C. PRODUCER and ARTIST mutually agree that in the event of any dispute of any nature where the monetary relief sought is $15,000 or less, both parties agree to mediated arbitration instead of traditional litigation. Arbitration will be held at a venue selected by mutual agreement in St. Louis County, Missouri, with a mediator decided by legal counsel of both ARTIST and PRODUCER.

Section 7: Execution.

Agreed to this 15th Day of May 2010.

_____

John Smith, Producer

_____

Jane Doe, Artist Representative

Finding a Good Lawyer

One of the most important investments you can make as a small business is to keep a lawyer on retainer. Since you're in a specialized business, it's also a great idea to find an attorney who practices in the area of entertainment law. Entertainment lawyers tend to have a keen interest in the music industry and generally will represent both major-label and independent artists on their way up (and down) in their careers. The advantages of having an expert with this kind of clout retained for your use are innumerable. This special relationship with a legal expert in the music industry will cost you—specialized attorneys tend to be more expensive than general practice—but having someone there who can explain the intricate legalities of copyright, publishing, distribution, and dealing with the complicated web of record label politics can be well worth whatever you have to pay.

Even if finding an attorney with specialized music industry experience is difficult, finding a good attorney you can trust for help with general business matters is very important and extremely helpful. You never know when you'll need a contract reviewed, help with negotiating terms with corporate or government clients, or—in a worst-case scenario—someone to help go after a client who breaks the terms of your contracts.

So how do you find a great attorney who meets your needs (and, most importantly, your budget)? First, check with your state bar association. Most state bar associations have great websites where you can search for attorneys in good standing and sort by specialized areas of practice to best suit your needs. Another great resource is Avvo (www.avvo.com), which allows you to search for attorneys based on many different criteria.

Once you've short-listed your choices, schedule appointments with them for a consultation; most attorneys will do this for no charge. There are a few questions you should always ask of any attorney you may be considering to keep on retainer:

- How much experience do they have in their chosen field of practice?
- Any notable clients or cases? (While attorneys cannot discuss specifics of most of their clients and their cases, many will have obtained permission from notable clients to use them as references for meetings such as this.)
- How much time do they personally dedicate to issues, both small and large, and how accessible are they for occasional questions and consultations?

- How willing are they to work within your budget limitations? Keeping a lawyer on retainer can cost a lot of money; in my case, my lawyer, with specialized entertainment experience, allowed me to retain him for a base fee of $250.

Marketing Materials

When I was in junior high school, I started my own business repairing computers. Back then, the Internet was barely in its infancy, and reaching out to potential customers meant hitting the pavement and distributing flyers and business cards. All of my advertising was in hard print form, and it wasn't cheap. It was hard work and required a lot of time, energy, and monetary investment to reach potential new customers. The times have certainly changed! While it's true that Internet promotion is now the way to go, especially in the social networking world of today, there are a few offline avenues you might want to consider investing in to promote your recording studio.

Business cards are one of the few old-school methods of advertisement that work really well. I frequently go to concerts and events with local musicians and I always hand my card out to anyone I meet, especially if we've had a great conversation about the recording industry or music technology. On my card, I list my name, phone number, e-mail address, and a website containing my portfolio and résumé. It's really easy to print business cards—many sites, including VistaPrint (www.vistaprint.com) offer professional-quality business cards for a very small investment. They'll even help you design your card if you don't already have something in mind.

Second, while posting flyers may seem very old school, they don't hurt. It won't cost much to print eye-catching, high-end flyers to promote your business, and it's something you should certainly consider. Posting your flyers where musicians are likely to see them is very important. Local coffee shops, music venues, and music equipment retailers will generally have no problem letting you post your materials on their bulletin boards. Old school or not, promotion is promotion, and exposure is always valuable.

Print ads may be expensive and considered redundant with good online marketing, but there're still a lot of people reading the paper—especially local fringe papers, which target the local artistic community. One of the most popular and expansive network of community media is run by Village Voice Media (www.villagevoicemedia.com), which has free local papers distributed in most major metro areas. Ad rates

Finding customers is hard—but finding where you might be able to connect with them isn't. In this worksheet, let's make a media list. This is your list of places you can reach out to and potentially advertise your business.

Local Culture Paper (entertainment magazines, papers that list live performances, music review papers, etc.): _____

_____

_____

College Papers: _____

_____

_____

Local Musician Blogs: _____

_____

_____

Local Music Review / Entertainment Writers: _____

_____

_____

Musician's Unions: _____

_____

_____

Local Jazz or Blues Societies: _____

_____

_____

are generally inexpensive, and these papers are always willing to help design a great ad for your use. Most of these publications cover the local music scene very well, and placement of your ad alongside local album reviews or local concert listings can go a long way toward exposing your studio business to potential clients.

And last, keep in mind: There's potentially a big market for your work outside of the music business, too. Many industries aren't as technologically connected as the music business (where promotion by social networking is extremely important, in contrast to corporate or government work). Networking with representatives of these industries will require, at the very least, a professional handshake and an offer of a business card.

In chapter 9, we'll dive headfirst into promotion via social networking—one of the most crucially important avenues of promotion in today's digital world.

Your Résumé and Demo Reel

As a working audio engineer, you're faced with the challenge of working in a field where, as the old saying goes, "the proof is in the pudding." Just like photographers, graphic artists, chefs, and other professionals who offer a tangible product from their creative endeavors, you'll be graded by potential clients (and industry peers alike) by your finished product and consistent quality work. It doesn't matter what equipment you use, where you record, what your background in audio engineering is, or how great you think your skills are. While it might sound harsh, if you can't prove that you can record, mix, and master a great recording, nobody will be interested in hiring you except low-tier customers who only care about the dollar amount spent on recording, not the ultimate sound quality. As an audio engineer with your own commercial studio, you should be focused on turning out unique, top-tier projects at every opportunity. So how do you best demonstrate this to your potential clients?

Making a demo reel is one of the most important things you can do as an audio engineer. A demo reel—a crossover term from the film industry—is your calling card, a tangible résumé of your best work that you can show off to potential clients. You should feature work that sounds exceptional, work that was recorded under unique circumstances, and/or a recording that did very well for your client's commercial interests.

Your demo reel can take a couple of potential forms. While the use of physical media in today's world seems like a dying trend, when making a demo reel on CD, you present a tangible product that your potential clients can judge your work on easily. Professionally printing simple, mastered disks is relatively inexpensive—for a short run of disks, around 100 to 500 units, you can expect to pay around one dollar per unit—and offers something that a potential client can use to evaluate your work on multiple playback systems (believe it or not, this makes a difference). You might also consider offering your demo reel on a cheap USB thumb drive. These, with a small amount of storage space, can be had relatively cheaply. Handing over your business card with a USB drive filled with a selection of your best material in MP3 format (or, better yet, uncompressed FLAC format) makes a great impression, but it's somewhat more expensive than printing CDs. Whichever method you go with to distribute physical copies of your demo reel, don't forget the huge importance of placing your demo material online. Even if your studio's website is very sparse, having a well-organized and easily downloadable demo reel is of high importance. When selecting audio to put on your demo reel, make sure you have your clients' permission to post the material—remember, even though you recorded it, the intellectual property still belongs to them.

Build Your Demo Reel

Bragging is one of the things that come most naturally to human beings. It's time to think of some of your glory moments so we can build your demo reel. This is something very important, as putting your best foot forward in your demo reel is one of the most important things that you as a new audio engineer can do.

Here's a list of potential ideas for recordings to include:

- Your first major client (or client who became significant later on)
- First major concert recorded
- Favorite song by any artist you've recorded
- Best production quality
- Best recording done with limited resources
- Best vocal tone on a recording you've done
- Best jazz or classical recording

05 Financial Planning and Management

So now that we've got a better idea of what your recording studio business will do, it's time to talk about the one subject that nobody likes to bring up: budgeting your money. While nobody understands your excitement more than a fellow recording engineer like myself, there are a few items of business you need to take care of between the time your studio is set up and when you book your first client. While it's tempting to look at a stack of recording gear and feel you're ready for your first client, there's a lot of behind-the-scenes work that still needs to be done. That includes the legalities of declaring yourself a business, insurance, and your pricing structures.

In this chapter, we'll talk about one of the most important things you need to start a business: money. Financing your business can be a complicated affair, and it's something that is generally a problem for most small businesses. Especially in today's turbulent economy, business lending is a challenging and complex issue; unfortunately, an overwhelming number of failing businesses have put business lenders in a bad position when it comes

Funding through Perseverance

One thing we'll be talking about is how limited business lending is these days. Since the economy collapsed leaving so many small businesses without any customers, many banks are simply not financing anything but the most well-qualified businesses. Don't let this discourage you—if you work at it, you'll be able to work your way up to building the credit your business deserves—and the credit it requires to operate.

to small-business lending. That being said, if you know what to look for, finding a financing system that works for your business might be a lot easier than you think.

Financing Your Dream

Assuming you haven't won the lottery or inherited millions from a relative, one of the unfortunate truths of starting your own business—even if it's home-based—is the fact that it's not cheap. You'll need to have enough money in the bank to pay for your equipment, to convert your space into something that works for your business needs, and to pay for all of the licenses and fees necessary for opening your business to the public. Not to mention the money you might need to pay for your personal needs.

There are a few types of methods you can use to fund your business, and they've all got advantages and disadvantages. It's up to you to decide which method for obtaining funding is the best for you, and you should base this decision on how profitable you think your business will be in the first few years. After all, taking on a loan with a repayment schedule you can't keep up with is one of the first mistakes many business owners make.

First, let's consider the easiest option: borrowing money from family or friends. Let's say you have a close friend or family member who's made some money for themselves and who wouldn't mind being an investor. The interest rate, if any, that you and your friend or family member agree upon will likely be quite a bit less than what you'll find with a bank (assuming you qualify for a loan at all). An added bonus is that your lender friend probably won't be running your credit score before agreeing to the loan.

While the idea of getting a loan from someone close to you might be attractive, don't get in over your head. Taking on a loan that you can't repay can cause some serious personal turmoil, especially if it's with a family member. You might want to consider "micro-lending" with these lenders instead—asking for loans of a couple thousand dollars or less, which could easily be repaid, even if things get rough. With larger loans you might end up in the challenging situation of defaulting on a loan given to you by somebody with whom you have a close personal relationship.

Another option is the traditional bank loan. These loans can come in many forms, depending on how your bank works. Even if your bank has liberal lending policies (and that's very rare these days), you'll be limited by your personal assets and credit score. Depending on the way you choose to legally operate your business, you might be able to obtain business lending in the name of the business itself, without your personal credit situation involved; however, this type of business financing is very difficult to get and is growing increasingly so. For now, let's talk about the methods in which you can obtain financing through a bank in your own name. This is your most likely way of getting the money you need, especially as a start-up business.

Personal, or Signature, Loans

If you want to get a line of credit under your own name and your personal credit score alone, you'll want to look for what's called a *signature loan,* sometimes simply called a *personal loan.* This is for a fixed amount of money, usually a compromise of a number you request during your initial visit to the bank. You'll have repayment terms that vary with the amount of the loan—larger loans will offer more expensive repayment terms, but with lower interest rates. These types of loans will require a cosigner if your personal credit isn't good, but require no collateral or established business assets in order to be approved. The best rates for these types of loans will come from local banks and credit unions.

Collateral, or Secured, Loans

Let's say your credit score isn't so great, and you don't have a cosigner who's able to offer their good credit as backing for your new endeavor. The next best way to finance your business is what's called a collateral loan, or secured loan. This type of loan is backed by something that you own outright—a home, car, property, or other tangible asset—and can be repossessed by the bank if you default on the loan. When signing a contract for this type of loan, you sign over the rights to the property you own to the bank on the condition that they are allowed to take ownership of the property if you fail to repay your loan as agreed. By doing this, the bank is relieved of some (or all) of their financial risk and liability in offering you the loan.

There are some good advantages to a secured loan. These types of loans typically come with a lower interest rate than an unsecured loan because the bank's risk is negated somewhat by the collateral property. And, in the case of default, you'll give up an asset—but chances are you won't be forced into bankruptcy to repay the loan.

Home Equity Loan

A popular type of collateral loan is a home equity loan; if you own your own home and have sufficient equity built up (that is to say, the value on your property has gone up, or you've paid off a large chunk of your original home purchase debt), you'll be able to take out a home-equity loan, which will give you access to a large chunk of money to pay for your business start-up expenses. If you'd prefer a revolving line of credit, you may wish to get a home equity line of credit instead; this loan is identical to a home equity loan, except you will receive access to an ongoing line of credit which you can draw from at any time, in any amount up to your full credit line. The difference here is that you'll have access to funds, but will not necessarily be responsible for paying back the full sum if you don't use it (similar to how a credit card operates). With a regular home equity loan, you receive the full lump sum, and must pay it back in full. These types of loans are especially risky for new businesses, even though the loan amount, interest rates, and the ease of approval might seem a lot easier (if your credit is halfway decent). Think about it: What's worse than closing your business and losing your home simultaneously? Certainly nothing I would feel comfortable thinking about.

That being said, if you're confident in your abilities to pay back the loan, a home equity loan may be quite helpful to you, especially if your personal credit score disqualifies you for a traditional personal loan with no collateral.

A Note about Credit Card Financing

If you choose to use credit cards for financing your business, think again. While the easy access to money (and a credit line you already have open) might make financing your start-up with a credit card look like a good idea, please watch out; many business owners have thought the same way, and ended up with loads of high-interest debt stacked atop growing monthly payments that they can't make. Credit cards usually offer the poorest interest rates in the business (unless you have exceptional credit and a spotless payment history). While credit cards aren't a bad idea for short-term purchases, you'll want to keep your initial investment away from these high-interest payments.

And if the thought of drowning in high debt while trying to manage a growing business isn't scary enough, here's a sobering fact: According to a 2009 Kauffman Firm Survey prepared at Monmouth University, for every $1,000 of outstanding credit card debt a business carries, their chances of failing as a business increases by 2.2 percent. Think about that before you pull out your plastic to fund your business.

Insurance and Licensing

When starting a business, it's important to factor in the costs of your business licensing alongside liability and property insurance. Both items are absolutely necessary—for both legal and logistical reasons.

One of the first things you should do is find a good, local insurance agent you can work with. While business insurance via the Internet is a great thing (and can sometimes save some additional money), I fully support the old-school method of dealing with someone locally, face-to-face. This person will be able to greater assess your unique needs as a home-based recording studio and will be able to give you the greatest amount of coverage that you need. And if you need to add certain temporary additions, or *endorsements,* to your insurance policy, having a good insurance agent you can call and explain the situation to can be incredibly valuable, especially if the agent understands your business. (And speaking of endorsements, why would you need to add one to your policy? For example, let's say you're doing a remote recording session and your equipment will be located inside a performance venue or rehearsal space for a period of time; calling your insurance agent to add this location as an endorsement will cover you in case of equipment loss at this location outside of your normal studio.)

As we've talked about—and I'm sure you know firsthand—recording is an expensive hobby, and an even more expensive business. Equipment will likely be your biggest expense and your biggest asset for your business in general. Insuring this equipment against loss—via theft, fire, flood, or worse—should be one of the first things you do before you open your studio for business. As with most businesses, the equipment you have is extremely important and critical to your survival. If your equipment disappears or goes down, you'll be in big trouble if you've got clients waiting for their projects to be completed. You'll also need to factor in the cost of protecting yourself and your business from unexpected liabilities, which can arise from accidents while customers are working in your facility. One lawsuit can easily sink a business and put you in financial ruin; insuring your business adequately can take this potential burden off your shoulders.

Liability Insurance

First off, let's talk about liability insurance. Liability insurance is insurance you purchase to cover your business in the event your business is negligent and causes injury or financial loss to another party. Liability insurance is necessary if you're bringing clients into your studio to record, even if you make all those who enter sign a waiver of liability. Unexpected things can happen, and liability insurance protects your business and personal assets if somebody decides to take you to court for any type of loss or injury sustained while visiting your place of business. While the individual coverage depends on your state and local laws, liability insurance is generally only for third-party claims (you can't file a claim against the business's insurance yourself), and only for claims that arise from outside individuals (employees, if you have any, are not covered), and you can't cover your own business equipment as part of it.

Liability insurance has two types of limits, one called your single-occurrence limit and another called your aggregate limit. Your single-occurrence limit is how much your insurance policy will pay on a single claim; you might find that this number is particularly low if you've chosen a less-expensive policy. Make sure you don't underinsure yourself by choosing a policy with a smaller single-occurrence limit. For example, a client may sustain an injury and sue you for $50,000 in damages; your single-occurrence limit might only cover $15,000. That's a big difference, and you'll be on the hook for the extra money, if the client refuses to settle. Your aggregate limit is how much, total, your insurance policy will cover over multiple claims (and let's hope that doesn't happen to you!). Keep in mind, policies with low limits will be cheaper, but could be potentially useless if something terrible happens at your business.

Property Insurance

The other type of business insurance you shouldn't go without is property insurance. While some of your items may be covered under your existing renter's or homeowner's policy, this type of insurance policy will comprehensively protect all of your business assets, along with those of clients visiting your studio. This is really important, as most of your clients will be bringing expensive musical instruments to the recording sessions.

Most of these insurance policies will cover a large range of events which could cause loss of equipment. These policies, called broad form policies, protect against a blanket list of loss-inducing events; fire, flood, and theft are the most commonly covered. From there, you can opt to add additional coverage, called specific or single-peril policies (also called single-peril riders). These cover situations not normally insured; it's a good idea to explore these additional policies, especially if you live in an area prone to unusual natural disasters such as earthquakes.

With most typical property insurance policies, your equipment will be covered in one of two ways. One is replacement value, which will insure the item for the actual cost your business will incur in replacing the item, regardless of how far depreciated the item is at the time of loss. For example, a brand new Shure SM57 microphone will cost you $99 to buy, brand new, while the depreciated, used value may be closer to $60 on a SM57 that you've been using in the studio. Your insurer will pay you the full, off-the-shelf retail value that you'd need to spend to replace the item. Unfortunately many less-expensive policies only cover actual cash value, in other words the depreciated amount your equipment is worth. That means that if the same $99 Shure SM57 is lost, you'll only receive the depreciated value to purchase a replacement with—and you'll have to make up the rest yourself. Obviously this can become very expensive.

Licenses

While you may have a killer studio setup, you're not officially a business in the eyes of the government if you're not properly licensed and don't have the requisite permits necessary for starting a business. This part of the business is not generally a very large expense, but one which you should always factor in to your initial budget. While I'd love to tell you exactly what you need, the requirements vary by state and municipality. Many states have unique requirements on the registration of a formal business. Your city may also require a business license, even if you're a sole proprietor. Depending on your local laws, you'll have to get a license to open your business from your local government. Fees may by state and city.

Resources on the Web

Because every state has different requirements, it's impossible to list every unique situation here. If you're looking for your state's legal requirements for opening a business, you can find links to every state's needs (and, many times, online registration) by visiting the following website: www.business.gov/register/licenses-and-permits.

Generally speaking, there are a few things every business will need to do before getting formal licensing. You'll need to first choose what type of business entity you want your business to operate under—whether you'll incorporate, be a limited liability corporation, or operate as a sole proprietor. This is an important decision, as it'll affect not only how your taxes are handled, but what liabilities you as the business owner can be held to.

You should certainly take the time to consult an attorney and a tax professional before choosing which way to establish your business. While the following information is offered as a baseline to give you information on your options, only a trained professional can give you the best advice for your particular situation. That being said, let's take a look at each of these types of businesses.

Sole Proprietorship

Being a sole proprietorship is one of the simplest ways to go into business for yourself. Many times, you won't even need to register your business with the government as a sole proprietor (but check with your local government first). Aside from registering as a sole proprietor, you'll generally also file a statement of fictitious name or business alias with your state government, which ties your name to a business name that you'll use, even if your business simply goes by your name. Being a sole proprietor means that you and your business are one entity. This is especially noteworthy as it exposes you to the sole financial and legal liabilities of your business. For example, debts in the name of your business will affect your personal credit, and all business credit approvals will be made based on your personal credit situation alone. You will use your social security number as the tax identification number for your business and will file your taxes as a sole proprietor, paying self-employment taxes. This makes your bookkeeping remarkably simple. Running your business as a sole proprietorship will save you a great deal of frustration in the beginning, and allow you to focus less on business bookkeeping and more on providing a top-notch product to win over customers.

While being a sole proprietor is typically the easiest way to start a business, especially when it comes to money, the disadvantages of opening as a sole proprietor are mainly financial, too. Being a sole proprietor is weighed against you when it comes time to apply for business credit. Most lenders won't accept a business unless it's established as a corporation or limited liability company. Keep this in mind if you don't have good access to working capital and can't get approved for many loans with your personal credit score. There's also the issue of liability. As a sole proprietor, you're on the line if anything happens. Hopefully, your business will be successful—but this also places stress on you as the business owner, especially if something happens that's the fault of your business operations. There's no dividing line between your business and your personal assets, which makes both fair game for a lawsuit involving your business.

Incorporation and Limited Liability Companies

When you're ready to move things up from being a sole proprietor, it's time to consider becoming either a corporation or a limited liability company. Both are much more complex than being a sole proprietor and require more paperwork and larger fees to establish. That being said, depending on your financial situation you may find that a corporation or LLC is a much better legal structure for your business than working as a sole proprietor.

Let's talk about corporations first. Incorporating is generally overkill for a small, home-based business, but it's an option you might wish to consider. Incorporating is generally the most expensive business licensing you can pursue because it requires a fairly complex legal process. Quite simply, a corporation is a business entity that's established completely separately from its owners—with its own legal obligations, privileges, and liabilities—and exists to serve a careful balance of everybody involved, including employees, creditors, and owners (called *stakeholders*). You'll need to file articles of incorporation with your state government, which will state information about the company and its assets (including who's in charge of legally running the company).

Incorporating is beneficial because it offers a very clear separation between personal assets and liabilities and those of the business. A corporation issues stock, whether public or private, and is required to maintain vast internal records—something you may not exactly want to tackle yourself. There's also the issue of taxes; as a corporation, your business will be taxed as the separate entity that it is, and you'll also be liable for personal taxes on your personal salary. That means, for a small one-man operation, you'll be paying double taxes. If you do choose to incorporate, please contact an attorney with extensive experience in business entities. While it's a relatively simple concept, there are several different kinds of incorporation structures you can choose. Becoming a corporation can be costly—upwards of $1,000, not including attorney's fees.

A limited liability company, or LLC, has many of the advantages of a corporation, without the tangled web of corporate paperwork and regulations. Like a corporation, an LLC is its own legal entity, and an LLC also keeps your individual assets separate from your business liabilities in most cases. The biggest advantages are in terms of taxation; in most areas, an LLC is what's called a transparent entity, or pass-through entity. Like being a sole proprietor, your profit (or loss) is entered onto your personal taxes and you're not required to file separate business taxes (or any of the more complicated corporate paperwork you see with a corporation). There are exceptions: In the District of Columbia, LLCs are treated just the same as corporations in terms of being taxed as their own entity. Many times LLCs can be filed online with minimal hassle—all it takes is a credit card.

Business versus Personal Finances

One of the biggest mistakes I made when starting my business was not keeping my business and personal finances separate. We've been talking about financing your business, which many times will equal a large chunk of money being deposited into a bank account. In my case, I received my loan check from my bank and promptly deposited it into my personal checking account. Seeing several thousand dollars added to your bank account can be a very uplifting experience—it can also tempt you to spend this money on things that don't relate to your business. When you've got an excess of money, it's easy to not pay attention to your spending, and before you know it, you're spending business money for personal purchases. Not a good situation! Aside from curbing the temptation to spend money that you'll need later for business expenses, keeping your business and personal finances separate will also help with your bookkeeping.

Be sure to establish a business checking account. Business accounts generally will require you to present your business license and articles of incorporation (or sole proprietor information; generally, your social security number and statement of fictitious name registration from your state government will do).

A business checking account offers two distinct advantages. One, you're able to keep all of your business transactions, including expenses and income, in one central location. This is a great thing, especially when tax season rolls around—you won't have to go far to find out how much money you made (or lost) in any given year. Two, having your own business bank account is generally the prerequisite to obtaining business credit. No matter what type of credit you plan to apply for—more on this later—a business bank account is generally a necessity. Having an account in your business name also gives you credibility with customers and vendors.

When it comes to credit spending, it's always a better idea to establish credit accounts in the name of your business, once you're established enough to do so; the reason being, if you've shielded yourself from liabilities by incorporating or forming an LLC, your individual assets cannot become part of debt collection activities.

Don't Forget Your Taxes

While it might be tempting to avoid the issue of taxes as a small business, doing things right from the start will help you greatly later on.

As in licensing your business, every state has different requirements for how a business such as your recording studio will be taxed. It might not be a huge amount of money to pay, but chances are you'll have some tax expense—or tax liability—if you're making money at your business. Aside from this, you'll also be liable for your individual self-employment taxes (if filing as a sole proprietor or LLC). Self-employment income up to $102,000 is taxed at a rate of 15.3 percent, with 12.4 percent of this tax going to social security and 2.9 percent to Medicare.

We'll talk more about taxes in chapter 7, but for now, keep in mind that you'll need to set aside part of your business income to pay these taxes, lest you be caught without a net when tax season rolls around.

Your Rate: Hourly Versus Flat Fee?

As a recording studio that's accepting new clients, at some point in the negotiation process, you'll need to figure out how much you need to charge in order to make a profit. How you decide to charge clients should depend on a number of factors.

First, how much are your services worth? There's really only one benchmark for this—what clients in your area are willing and able to pay. While you might believe your skills to be worth a great deal of cash, you might need to keep yourself in check. If your studio can't compete with the big guys in town, you can't charge a rate anywhere near what they charge, and if the equipment you're recording on isn't giving industry-standard results, that will affect how much you can charge, too. Still, in today's digital age, a modest investment in equipment can get you very close to what the big guys can do—at a much more reasonable price. Also, with the studio being located in your home, you'll have a much lower overhead than any studio running in a large commercial space.

Second, research your competition. Find out what the other studios in town charge for similar products, and find out how your studio stacks up against theirs. It's not fair for you to charge the same rate that a large commercial facility offers if your end result can't compare. While I'm sure you've put a great deal of thought into your studio setup, if you can't deliver results that are both industry-standard ("radio ready" as they say), you're not going to get the same type of business. If you're just producing demos for local bands with little commercial appeal, your rate can be fairly low, as long as you're still covering what little overhead you have and are making a profit for yourself.

This particular issue is one that really causes problems for most home recording studios. If you price your services too low, you risk classifying yourself as an amateur operation, something you really don't want to do. There's a reason the guys running a small hard-disk recorder in the corner of a bedroom only charge $15 or $20 per hour: The quality they're getting isn't worth much more. In your studio, I'm assuming you've made a significant investment in your equipment, and you've got a product that can easily compete with whatever your biggest competitor can provide.

For most larger projects, I tend to favor a flat-rate pricing schedule. While it may seem like an easy way to overextend myself for lower pay, it's generally more fair to my client in the long run and allows me to take the client's individual needs into account, along with their budget. It's certainly not all about the client: It also makes it very easy to budget your expenses for a single project, as you'll know up front how much to expect, whereas most hourly projects add up over time. I'll offer the recording, mixing, and mastering for a single price, payable throughout the course of the project. It's up to you to decide how you want your clients to pay. Personally, I ask for 50 percent up front, with monthly payments of the rest throughout the course of the project, with the master delivered only after the final payment is made (and cleared). Never, under any circumstances, give out a usable product before getting paid in full.

As I mentioned, flat-rate pricing can present a problem for you as the business owner if you underquote your project. For flat-rate projects, you should always be specific about how much of your time you're willing to include for this price; don't leave it open-ended. From personal experience, this can sometimes be a disaster. A few years ago, I gave a flat-rate estimate to a local band, thinking the project wouldn't take more than ten hours of tracking along with a few hours' worth of mixing. How wrong I was! The band was unprepared to work in the studio, and I

Flat-rate versus Hourly Pricing Structure

When you're bidding on a project with a client, you need to figure out if you want a flat-rate or an hourly price. Both have distinct advantages for both you and the client, and it's sometimes hard to figure out which you should use. Here's a guide to the pros (+) and cons (−) of hourly vs. flat-rate projects.

HOURLY:

+ Allows for shorter projects to be done in a small amount of time; generally voice-overs and short mixing sessions.

+ Gives a client the ability to budget for a longer-term project on a lower budget.

+ Allows the client to buy just as much time as they can afford throughout the life of the project.

− Makes it harder to land longer-term but small-budget projects.

− Depending on your hourly rate, may make you uncompetitive to larger operations in town.

FLATRATE:

+ Is best for large projects that will take a significant portion of time.

+ Generally more fair for clients and yourself, as long as you estimate correctly.

+ Allows you to budget precisely for how much revenue a single project will bring.

− Not good for smaller, low-budget projects.

− An easy way to overextend and underbill yourself, unless you know how the recording process will work in great detail.

ended up having to push higher-paying projects out of the way in order to make room for them. If I had been up-front with how much time I was willing to dedicate to the project at that rate, this would have been avoided, as I could have easily asked for more money to compensate for the extra time I had to put into the recording process. In the end, the album took nearly two years—when I originally planned on dedicating around six months of time to finishing completely. I stood by the contract and the band only paid their original quote. I took a huge hit making sure this project got to the finish line, not something I'm in any hurry to repeat.

While a flat rate works best for large projects that require a considerable amount of time, for some projects an hourly rate may make more sense—such as those for corporate or government clients and clients who need simple mixing and mastering work. I tend to live by the rule that any project that will require twenty-four hours or less of studio time will go hourly; a larger flat-rate pricing break may not make sense for these smaller projects.

In chapter 9, we'll talk about another difficult pricing problem for home-based recording studios: when to charge a fair market price and when to give the music industry's favorite discount, the "hook-up."

Financing for Your Clients

One of my dirty secrets in life is that I spent a couple of years playing guitar in a touring band. It's not a job I particularly enjoyed, especially compared to my role in the music business now, as an audio engineer. In those two years, though, I learned a great deal about the inner workings of musicians—and one sad fact is that most of them don't make a whole lot of money.

While it's a great day when a major or indie-label project comes your way with a fully loaded expense account, the vast majority of your clientele will probably come from local or regional musicians. Being in one of these bands is an exceptional challenge; a feat that should be applauded. As a live sound engineer, I work firsthand with a lot of bands and see how much they bring in from an average gig—it's not encouraging.

Sadly, when it comes to supporting yourself full time with music, most musicians don't do too well. That means that the majority of your clientele will come to you with one story or another as to why they can't afford your services. And believe me, nothing is more discouraging than realizing that your entire livelihood is based on an industry that doesn't make much money throughout the first few tiers of success.

Offering financing to credit-worthy clients is a fantastic move to make. Giving your clients the ability to finance their studio work over a period of time will generally present you more clients since coming up with a chunk of money is hard for most bands. When it comes to choosing a financing package, there are multiple ways you can go about it. Whichever method you choose, make sure you understand the benefits and risks thoroughly; after all, the only true method to make sure you always get paid is to accept full payment up front.

- **Offer in-house financing.** This can be done a couple different ways—you can come up with a payment amount (and interest rate, if any) and accept payment in cash, or you can go with a financing company that handles this for you. Your client will go directly through your lending partner, who will pay you for the service in full (minus a servicing fee). Whatever method you choose, make sure your client is good for it; while a default by your client won't directly affect you if you choose a third-party lender (you get paid ahead of time), it's probably not smart to set your client up to drown in debt if they can't afford it in the first place. American General Lending is one company worth looking into, as they're known to be used by artists to finance projects.

- **Accept credit cards.** Setting up a merchant account is a somewhat expensive proposition for most small businesses, but it's worth it to be able to accept plastic if a majority of your clients wish to pay this way. You'll need a business bank account, and in order to set up the actual merchant account, you also must present your business license information. The fees are sometimes on the high side—you often have to pay a monthly maintenance fee (called a *gateway fee*), transaction fees (a small, fixed fee per transaction—somewhere around twenty to thirty cents), and a monthly "statement fee" (around $10 per month). Aside from the fees, the merchant account will keep a percentage of each transaction, which can be as high as 3 percent. You'll also have to make a minimum amount of transactions per month in order to keep your account (and if you don't meet this number, you have to pay the difference out-of-pocket—usually around $25). However, the extra business you'll get from being able to accept credit cards can easily outweigh the fees, if enough customers decide to use them.

- **Use alternate options for accepting credit cards.** Setting up a PayPal business account (www.paypal.com) can allow you to accept credit card payments for your clients easily, securely, and with fees competitive with using a traditional merchant account. It's especially a good idea for small businesses, as you may not make enough credit card sales to keep your fees low. There are also more high-tech options to the standard credit card terminal, too: Companies like ProcessAway offer iPhone apps to easily and securely accept credit card payments through your mobile phone.

Sample Billing Contract

If you've chosen to allow a client to pay over time, here's a simple contract you can use to make sure your clients pay on time. While this is separate from the original service contract, it's equally important. It's a document that allows your client to understand that you're serious about collecting payments from them in a timely manner.

Again, a warning about using this contract as your own: while I'm perfectly fine with you using this however you like, please check with a trusted attorney to make sure it's within the guidelines for your local and state laws.

Full or Part Time?

When deciding to start a business, it's really tempting to dive headfirst into the everyday operations of your business. Unfortunately, the financial realities of being dependent upon your new venture to support yourself might not be in your favor at first. Being self-employed is an adventure like no other—you're in charge of every aspect of your daily routine and your success is tied directly to the amount of hard work and street-level hustle you do. You should be prepared to put in a great deal of time running your business.

Remember in chapter 1 we talked about how much time most self-employed people put into their work on a weekly basis? It's staggering to think about working more than forty hours a week at a business alongside a second job to make ends meet. But what's a good indication that you're ready to fully quit your day job and run your recording studio full-time?

There's no hard- and fast-answer, because it depends on every person's unique situation. Do you have a large cushion of money to fall back on? Will your basic needs—housing, food, utility bills, car payments, insurance (for your home, car, and business), and business loan payments—be taken care of by your income alone? For most small business owners first starting out, that answer is no. And you might be lulled into a false sense of financial security by having a large chunk of your business loan money still in the bank. Remember, that money isn't necessarily for sustaining you personally—it's for your business needs.

The bottom line is this: If you can't afford to fully support yourself on your business income alone, it's probably not a good idea to go full-time right away. Don't

Direct Payment Agreement

I, Jane Doe, representative of the band SAMPLE BAND, hereby agree to a payment schedule with John Smith, d/b/a John Smith Sound, located in St. Louis, MO, as follows:

A. Grand total of $1,800 as defined in the previously agreed contract.

B. A deposit of $600 will be secured as a nonrefundable deposit on recording time and services, with the remaining balance paid, as agreed, on the 1st and 15th of every month.

C. Payments will be debited via credit card on the 1st and 15th of every month until full balance is paid, unless prior arrangements are made.

D. In the event a payment is declined by the credit processor and not made in a timely manner, all work on SAMPLE BAND's project will be halted. Work will be reinstated once all arrears are paid in full and arrangements to pay the remaining balance are made.

E. All conditions in the original contract apply.

Agreed to this day, June 1, 2010.

_____

Jane Doe

feel bad, and don't feel like you're a failure. You can't be expected to take a gigantic financial loss and potentially let your important bills slide—it's not smart for you or for those you support. And keep this in mind: Even the best studios have a lot of downtime, and a majority of your clients will also have day jobs and want to work on their projects during evening or weekend hours. This is great for you, as a new recording studio owner; you likely will have more than enough time to keep a part-time day job to help meet your financial obligations.

So are you ready to go full-time, or stay part-time? Ask yourself the following three questions:

- What are your financial needs? This includes all of your monthly bills for both you personally and your business. You'll probably have to tighten your belt on spending.
- How much money do you have in your personal savings account? You should have enough saved to cover at least one year's worth of bills; many resources suggest two years' worth of savings.
- How much business do you realistically expect? If you don't have a broad base of clients to choose from, becoming a self-sustaining business is going to be a very hard thing to accomplish.

While everybody's personal situation is different, the stress that can come from starting a new business is intense. Late hours and a lot of hard work will be the norm—and not everybody's cut out for that. While I know you'll be working hard to establish your studio, take a piece of advice from someone who's been there: Don't let yourself fall into a bad financial situation because you don't want to go part-time when you need to. It will profoundly affect your personal life and your mental health. Take it slow and let your business grow organically; you'll know when it's right to go full-time.

06

Outfit Your Studio

Audio production and engineering is a vocation for "gearheads"—if you didn't love the latest and greatest in audio gear, you wouldn't be in this job. Now that we've talked about some of the more mundane business details, let's get down to what you're probably most excited about: outfitting your studio.

Unfortunately most of us have to adhere to budgets when setting up our businesses, and it's sometimes startling to look at your budget after your initial business expenses are paid and realize you've still got some gear to buy. I fell victim to this, too—and quickly found myself needing to scramble to obtain a second business loan to cover some equipment costs I hadn't factored in. Making sure you've stuck to your budget so far will make things go much smoother.

In this chapter, we'll talk about selecting your space and outfitting it with the proper equipment for your business. Aside from the gear, we'll also talk about creating the right acoustic environment to keep your clients (and your neighbors) happy. Here's where the fun part starts!

Finding Your Space

While most home-based businesses can be operated from a small home office—wherever that may be—running a recording studio from your home is going to require a lot more space. You'll also need to make sure that your recording area has access to clean power, and, most importantly, good acoustics. Consider this: Most musicians have access to fairly good recording software and can produce a decent demo recording at home. What truly will set you apart (other than your great engineering skills) is having a professional space in which to record. You might also want a separate area to work with your clients in preproduction meetings, or a lounge area for musicians who aren't actively tracking at that moment to relax while others in the band work. While it may be tempting to put your studio in a small spare bedroom or in the corner of your basement, you'll need much more space committed to the studio in order to meet the needs of most of your paying clients. Keep in mind that with today's technology, many musicians can record in their bedrooms for free—if they're going to pay you, you need to have suitable conditions to make the transition from home to a paid studio worth their time (and money). Let's take a look at exactly what you'll need, depending on the type of studio you plan on running.

If you have access to a basement, this generally makes the best space for a recording studio. It's isolated from the rest of the goings-on in the home and can be easily fitted with whatever you need to produce the proper acoustic spaces. Basements also have one important acoustic aspect going for them—they're underground, which generally provides isolation from outside noises (from personal experience I can tell you that, while it may sound cool, I guarantee that an improperly timed airplane approach to a nearby airport can ruin a good take). If you don't have a basement available, go for the next available large space that you can efficiently treat acoustically. A garage can work for this purpose, but most garages weren't designed with good insulation in the walls or roof. While garage spaces can work well as control rooms and live recording rooms, you may want to build a separate isolation room attached to your garage space.

The smallest and easiest setup for any studio is a vocals-only setup. This arrangement is best suited for just mixing, recording hip-hop vocals and hip-hop production, and voice-over recording. In this case, you'll need two separate areas: a control room and a live room or isolation booth. Your control room will be where the majority of your recording equipment is stored, and where you as the engineer will do most of your work. This room will have your recording and mixing components and your outboard equipment. It will be acoustically treated to provide a fairly flat, neutral response in the room so that your monitoring setup can properly reproduce what you're working on at the moment. This room will also need to be isolated from your live room, because as the engineer, you'll need to listen critically to the recording as it takes place. Having everything take place in one open room offers absolutely no advantage over the standard bedroom studio that your clients can easily set up for themselves with even the most modest budget.

Control Room Basics

- Your control room is the heart of your studio; this is where your recording gear lives. This room is where you record, mix, and master your projects. It's the brain of your studio and where the magic will (hopefully) happen.
- You'll want good acoustic treatment, but not necessarily isolation. This room will be where you monitor your recordings via studio monitors, and while having a good response here helps, save the money to put toward perfecting the acoustics in your live rooms. The biggest problem you could potentially run into with this room's acoustic properties is leakage. You don't want to leak into your live room or the other rooms in your home.
- Have sufficient space for your recording setup; whether you're completely in-the-box with a computer, or using an outboard control surface along with preamps, compressors, and EQ, you'll need to have plenty of room for everything, including studio monitor speakers. Given today's modern equipment, you'll be very surprised at what you can fit into a small room.
- Proper storage in your control room should be dedicated to microphones, cables, and headphones. Consider keeping your valuable microphone collection under lock and key; when people rob recording studios, microphones are usually the first items they go for as they're small, portable, and relatively valuable considering their small size.

Control Room Checklist

- ❏ Does the room offer good isolation from other areas of your home and from neighbors?
- ❏ Is there room for the equipment you require in your control room?
- ❏ Is sufficient power located in the control room?

Aside from your control room, you'll need at least one live room. A live room is the actual space the person you're recording will work in. If you're only doing vocal recording, this room doesn't have to be large—just enough space to fit one or two people comfortably. In the recording industry, we call this type of room an isolation booth. This live room will need to be connected to your control room with both audio tie lines (for input, with typically XLR connectors for microphones and output, via either a headphone amplifier fed by your recording snake or a wireless monitoring feed) and power (for lighting, small musical instrument amplifiers, and recording devices that might require a power feed, such as tube microphones). Isolation rooms are called such because they're truly isolated from the surrounding areas, and acoustically near perfect. You'll want this room to be as absolutely dead as possible, and void of any interference and noise from the outside. This room will be for recording critical, precision items such as the human voice; keeping away outside noise is one of the things a professional studio can offer that sets it apart from a bedroom-demo studio that many musicians have.

Building this room is, most times, a challenge. Homes weren't designed with perfect acoustics in mind, especially the kind of isolation we're looking for. Isolation rooms can easily be made out of walk-in-size closets, and they can also be readily crafted in a corner of any given room, especially basements (where you have a floor above you; believe it or not, this allows you to easily construct what's called a "room within a room" to make near-perfect isolation a reality). If you're in a rented home, converting this space can be an even bigger challenge because of existing restrictions by the property owner.

Isolation Room Basics

- This room should be a separate room from the control room area; all recording and mixing equipment should be in a separate room to reduce noise pollution of your signal.
- Your isolation room should be as acoustically dead as possible; treat this small room the best you can to prevent outside noise and interference. You should be able to record a vocal track or acoustic guitar track from this room without any outside noise affecting the clarity and fidelity of your recording.
- This room will need to be connected to your control room. While being connected physically is a good idea (being able to see your recording musicians for cues is extremely useful), as long as you can run sufficient audio lines to your isolation room you should be fine.

From here, you can expand based on what your projected needs will be. Do you plan on recording full bands? Then you'll need to have both your isolation room (for vocals, small acoustic instruments, and isolated amplifiers) along with a large live room with suitable space and acoustics to record, at minimum, a full drum kit. This room should have acoustic treatment to lessen the room's effect, unless your room naturally sounds fantastic. Some of the world's best live rooms aren't acoustically perfect, but offer an aesthetically pleasing acoustic sound. Chances are, whatever room you choose to use will be fine, with a few adjustments.

Commercial Studio Essentials

So other than a good acoustic space, what sets the little guys apart from the big names in recording?

There are two things that will set smaller studios apart from the big guys, and both are things you can focus on to give yourself an edge over larger operations in your area. One is the skill of engineering; there are some great studio engineers out there that do unbelievable things with fairly simple equipment. This type of engineering skill doesn't come overnight, but spending a great amount of time honing your skills in many different situations is one way you can easily set yourself apart from the pack. While many large commercial operations have great engineers on staff, most clients in your projected price range will not be working with the A-list engineering talent. Chances are, most of their tracking will be handled by interns and staff who've just recently graduated from internships to full engineering positions. The A-list talent costs a lot of money, many times more than what you're charging. By taking your engineering skills to the next level, you'll be able to attract better clients and more work. Consider taking professional certification classes to give you an edge; for example, while many engineers know how to use Pro Tools, there are very few with full-on professional training.

The other area you can focus on is equipment. While many commercial studios have industry-standard equipment, many of them offer access to vintage gear that only the highest-paying clientele can afford to make use of in their recordings. If your studio can offer something unique, you stand a much better chance at setting yourself apart. How about a Pro Tools–based digital studio with top-notch analog summing for mix-down? A studio that offers something different, something unique, can go a long way, especially in a budget, home-based operation.

Still, there are a few basics that all studios should be sure to have. As a commercial studio, you have to maintain the highest commercial standards possible. That means that you can't get by with a simple setup as if it was your personal demo studio; a sixteen-track all-in-one hard-disk recorder won't cut it. While it means spending more money, you need to be able to offer access to industry-standard software packages

Audio Recording Software

AVID Pro Tools (latest version, either HD or LE, depending on your hardware configuration) and Apple Logic Studio. These two software packages are the most widely used packages; chances are you'll be using Pro Tools as your main recording and mixing platform. If you have these software tools in your arsenal, you will be able to take in 98 percent of client projects that were started in home studios (or finish mixing projects started in other commercial establishments). One of the most important things to remember is compatibility. As we talked about earlier, being compatible with other commercial and project-grade studios is extremely important. Clients will often bring you projects on a USB drive and ask you to start your project based off of this demo session. Compatibility with the latest version of both Pro Tools and Logic will accomplish this. Remember, you'll need Pro Tools hardware to use Pro Tools; Logic will work with your built-in audio interface, and you can always port the session over to Pro Tools for mixing and editing.

Software Plug-Ins

The most important piece of software you can have in your recording plug-in arsenal is Antares Auto-tune. This is not an expensive piece of software (at the time of this writing, a full-featured copy costs $599 via the Antares website). Auto-tune is the essential, industry-standard pitch correction tool used by a vast majority of commercial recording engineers to correct off-pitch vocals, or to manipulate vocals and instruments for effect purposes. This software is immensely popular, and even if your personal engineering ethic steers you clear of using Auto-tune, your clients may think differently and request this software to be used for specific reasons on their project. And making the customer happy is the number one goal, right?

Two-Track Editing

Most recording studios will also need a two-track editor. These software packages allow linear editing of stereo files for mastering purposes. While you can easily do linear editing in Pro Tools or Logic, it's a lot easier with a dedicated two-track editor where you can swap back and forth between tracks very easily, and still use all of your same plug-ins for mastering.

for both recording and mix-down, and you'll also need to offer several options for microphones when recording. One microphone doesn't work for everything!

So let's look at a few items that you'll need to include in your home recording studio. Even though it may not be the cheapest list of items, you'll be glad you have them. These are all items that are industry standard in all commercial recording studios, and without them you may have a hard time attracting professional clients.

Microphones

Microphones are the next area that sets the little guys apart from the big commercial operations. Microphones can be very expensive, but with a few select purchases, you can equip your studio with world-class microphones that will give your clients the sounds they want with minimal investment on your part. Many times a good microphone locker will be the hallmark of a great studio—and something that brings your clients back for more. Remember your recording process, though; even if you have the best microphone in the world (and let's not start the debate on which one that is!), a bad-sounding instrument or bad vocal take will still sound bad. Work with your clients to take the time to prepare their instruments for recording before worrying about which microphone to use.

One of my favorite commercial studios offers an unbelievable array of microphones; from Coles ribbon microphones to the famous AKG C12, this studio has absolutely everything I could want. Unfortunately it also comes with a really high hourly rate, even for freelancers buying time as independent contractors. Having those microphones is great, but for most of your clients, you won't need such overkill. See page 76 for a selection of the microphones I find absolutely indispensable for recording; you may find different microphones meet your needs, but in my experience a vast majority of my clients have absolutely no problems getting a sound they like with the following selection on hand. All of these choices are relatively affordable, and you may be able to save money by buying these microphones used, too.

Room Acoustics 101

As we get into this section, let me apologize ahead of time—this is probably the most technologically complicated chapter, and I know from experience that I can't give you an exact assessment or plan of action for your recording space's acoustic situation without actually being there. With the information in this section, you'll learn why treating your room's acoustics is important—and why soundproofing

Drum Recording

Kick Drum: Sennheiser E901, Shure Beta 91, Heil PR-40, Shure Beta 52, Beyer M-88

Snare Drum: Heil PR-22, Shure Beta 57, Beyer M-201

Toms: Sennheiser E604, Sennheiser E609, Shure Beta 98, Sennheiser MD421

Overheads, High-Hat: Heil PR-30, Shure SM-81, AKG C414 (or the less-expensive, cardioid-only C214), Earthworks SR-30

Guitar Amplifier Recording

Cascade FatHead II, Shure SM-57, Shure SM-7B, Heil PR-30, Sennheiser E609

Vocal Recording

Rock: Shure SM-7B, Heil PR-40, AKG C414

Voice-Over: Heil PR-40, Neumann TLM103, Neumann U87I

Singer-songwriter, folk: AKG C414, Neumann U87I

Acoustic Instrument Recording

Neumann KM184, Neumann KM140, Shure SM81, Earthworks SR-30, AKG C414, AKG C480B

is a different, more complicated, and more expensive endeavor. If you're building your space from scratch, only you and a qualified professional can determine what soundproofing avenues you'll be able to explore, given your budget. It's an expensive, complicated, and relatively invasive process. For now, let's focus on learning the basics of acoustics, and the best way to treat your space.

We'll talk in this section about how to properly treat the three kinds of rooms you need for a simple studio setup: a control room, a live room, and an isolation room.

As I mentioned before, the best rooms for recording depend on what you're recording, and as we've talked about, for recording bands, you'll need one live room and one isolation room, along with your control room. Once you've identified the space for your recording studio, here's where you'll really need to work hard to achieve good results: soundproofing your room and treating your room's acoustics. Keep in mind, soundproofing and acoustic treatment are not the same thing. True soundproofing may not be an option for you—more about this later.

Most rooms were not designed with superior acoustics in mind. A lot of hard surfaces, a lack of absorbing materials, and a generally awkward geometry can make a room—no matter how visually appealing—sound terrible. This has been the case in a great number of rooms that I've seen while consulting with potential studio builders, and it's one of the most frustrating, time-consuming, and budget-busting things you'll have to tackle in your business. One of the benchmarks of a fine recording studio is the ability to have both an isolated, dead-sounding room for vocals and acoustic instruments, and a live room with unique acoustics suitable for larger groups—at minimum, a live drum kit. When deciding where in your home to build your studio, acoustics should be one of the first things you think about.

Sound itself consists of acoustic waves, which are physical oscillations that occur when something—be it a musical instrument, a speaker, or a human vocal cord—creates vibrations of varying magnitudes, called hertz, which are the number of oscillations, or cycles, per second. The more cycles, the higher the frequency range. Human hearing, in a perfect situation, generally has the capability of intelligibly discerning between 20 Hz and 20 kHz—a fairly wide range of potential sound. The human ear can't pick up much below 20 Hz (and, over time, your high-end response will dull, thanks to exposure-related hearing loss and the natural progression of age). Bone conduction—where vibrations are transmitted through your bone structure to your nerves, including auditory structures—allows us to experience acoustic vibrations far below what we can hear.

Why is this knowledge important for room acoustics? Sound of varying oscillations travels at different speeds, and it doesn't simply disappear when it hits a hard surface. Sound will generally do one of two things when it meets a surface: It can bounce off of the surface and go back into the room at a lessened magnitude, in different directions; or, it can be absorbed, in which case any bouncing reflections are minimized or eliminated.

As a home-based recording studio engineer, you've got one major potential issue to deal with. When sound strikes a surface, it can also use the surface it comes in contact with to retransmit the sound waves back into the room. If you've ever lived in a multifamily housing situation such as an apartment, you've likely experienced this phenomenon in the form of loud bass notes vibrating through your walls. What might surprise you is that the overall volume in the other person's home may not be as loud as you think; many types of building materials are excellent transmission vehicles for sound, and since lower frequencies require fewer cycles per second to transmit, they can easily come across loud and clear. This is obviously a big issue if you have close-by neighbors, because they won't be happy with constant noise coming from both your live room and your control room.

If you live in a rented home, chances are you won't have much leverage to actually soundproof your space. True soundproofing accomplishes one thing: It stops the transmission of sound waves outside of the soundproofed room by cutting off their vehicles of transmittal. Sound is transferred through air and can easily transmit through neighboring structures and repropagate on the other side of a wall, for example—usually your neighbor's if you live in an apartment or condo. Depending on your unique acoustic situation, this might require building a room within a room, which uses trapped air as insulation against transmission. Like I said, it's costly and invasive, but if you're going through the trouble of building from scratch, soundproofing is the best way to go.

Before you go into installing acoustic treatment, keep in mind that it's not always necessary to put acoustic treatment up at all. Some rooms sound fine on their own; don't feel like you need to treat acoustic problems that don't really exist. Only treat for glaring problems; don't reinvent the wheel. Some reverb and character can be great things in any live room.

The Materials of Acoustic Treatment

There are three kinds of materials that you will likely use: diffusers, foam, and bass traps.

First, let's talk about diffusers. Because different rooms have different characteristics, you might find that your room has buildups of certain frequencies, and a lack of frequency response in others. A great acoustic space has a relatively diffuse frequency response—meaning not overwhelming nor lacking in one frequency or another. Good diffusion can make a really small but well-tuned room sound amazing; it can make a large room sound well-controlled, warmer, and clearer.

As mentioned earlier, different frequencies resonate at different oscillations, and some surfaces will absorb and retransmit certain vibrations better than others. This creates unpleasant reflections and an unnatural buildup of certain frequencies in a room, all of which, in excess, is bad for recording.

Good diffusers are extremely expensive. Most low-priced ones work, but they require other treatment in addition. You'll usually install diffusers on the largest flat surface directly in the line of fire, usually the ceiling.

Acoustic foam is another item you'll use frequently. Acoustic foam simply absorbs frequencies—mainly high- and mid-range frequencies—which cause an unpleasantly reflective sound in a room. Acoustic foam is easy, cheap, and very effective, making it one of the most frequently used forms of acoustic treatment in the world. If you need to make an isolation room, covering the walls and ceiling of a closet will give you a fantastic live room for a very minimal investment.

When buying foam, stick to brands that are specifically designed for acoustic applications. Egg crate foam may seem effective, but it's not designed to be very capable in taming frequency response issues. Also, any specialized acoustic foam you buy should be flame-retardant. Most egg crate or packing foams are not, something you certainly don't want to deal with in the event of an emergency.

Bass traps do exactly what they say: They trap bass frequencies and both absorb and diffuse to tighten low-end response in the room. Since bass frequencies are generally bigger and more powerful than higher frequencies, bass traps must be built out of heavy-duty material, and are finely tuned for their specific purpose. Like diffusers, great-quality bass traps demand a high price.

Treating a Live Room or Control Room

Acoustically, your live room will be middle-of-the-road in terms of complexity of acoustic treatment required, and your control room will be much the same. Your live room is likely to be the biggest room of your studio setup—which further adds to the complexity of the acoustic situation. We'll start here, because once you have your live room ready to go, the rest will fall into place quickly.

First off, it's time to evaluate your acoustic situation. How does the room sound when you stand in the middle and clap your hands? Listen closely—can you hear the reflections of your handclaps bouncing off the surfaces in the room? If so, you need some acoustic treatment. If you can hear something as low-velocity as your hands clapping together, just think about what you'll deal with when you have a drum kit or guitar amp blaring. You want this room to be clean-sounding, yet retain as much of its character as possible. Since most of the things you record will be replicated using close-microphone techniques, this room doesn't need to be perfect.

Second, let's evaluate the existing materials in the room. Is it carpeted or solid flooring? Carpeting, generally, is a fantastic acoustic insulator, although it's not the most convenient for moving around and securing instruments, amplifiers, drums, and microphone stands. If it's solid flooring, bringing in a few rugs—enough to cover a significant portion of the floor—is a great idea. It'll give you a surface to set instruments on, and help deaden the reflections even further.

From there, you should turn your efforts to treating the walls and ceiling. As we talked about before, diffusers are a fantastic choice for ceiling treatment of larger rooms and your live room certainly qualifies. Installing these is a great idea if you notice a large reverb-like sound with little definition—this comes from the smearing of the room's frequency response due to reflections. Once you've controlled the reflectiveness, you may consider spot-treatment on the walls to help tame the high and high-mid frequencies if they're particularly harsh.

In the control room, you'll want a similar frequency response, but you may want to deaden the space a little more to assist in hearing your studio monitors loud and clear. You'll want to make sure you can get as absorbed in the mix as possible—and adding additional diffusers to your room will accomplish this.

Treating an Isolation Room

Making an isolation room is a very easy thing to do. Whether you choose to build a separate room in the corner of an existing room or convert a small closet, your goal is to make the space sound as acoustically dead as possible. The easiest thing to do? Cover almost every surface with professional-quality acoustic foam. It's a small room, and you won't need to do very much else. Just make sure you leave space to run, at the very least, one microphone cable and one headphone cable into the booth, along with electricity for both a light and any equipment of yours that might need it. It can be as easy as that!

Renting and Borrowing Gear

As you've gone into the process of making your studio perfect, you've probably spent a great amount of time pouring through professional audio catalogs wishing you had every piece of equipment possible for your studio. It's not economically feasible, especially if you have a limited budget. But sometimes, projects will require you to go outside of your studio to find equipment to perform specific functions for the project. In these types of situations, you should consider renting gear.

I'm a big fan of keeping good relationships with rental houses. Many of the best are located in Nashville, Tennessee, thanks to their booming music industry. They offer everything from microphones to compressors to vintage instruments, and it can all be on your doorstep in around twenty-four hours.

Renting gear is fun, but keep in mind, you'll need a credit card with available credit equal to the retail price of the rented item, at least until you have a good rapport with the rental company. They'll pre-authorize your card for the amount of the unit and then settle only the rental amount after the gear is returned safely. You'll also be expected to maintain liability insurance in case you break or lose the equipment. Still, it's a cost-effective option for buying all the toys you want but won't use enough to justify the cost.

Making Your Studio Unique

After you've set up the basics, let's go back to what we talked about earlier about market competition. Sadly many businesses fail because they can't keep up with the already established competition, either in quality, price, or both. However, if you've gotten this far, chances are you have a pretty good grasp of what your studio needs to make to survive. Now that the major purchases are out of the way, you can take time to find ways to make your studio unique. It might be easy—maybe the competition does a good job, but there's one thing their clients wish they did. It's your chance to jump in and offer a product or service that's just as good with more value for their dollar.

How can you stand out in a crowded market? Consider what's available in your recording space. Do you have a vintage or boutique microphone collection that makes your recordings sparkle in comparison, or some stellar analog outboard gear attached to your Pro Tools rig? How about a selection of great instruments for client use? All of these things add to your initial investment, but if you've got a magic trick up your sleeve to make exceptional recordings, by all means, write it into your budget. Also consider offering extra services. We'll talk about this in more detail later, but you might consider offering artwork services or digital distribution along with recording services. If a band can get a full package deal, it's all the better.

07

Taxes and Record Keeping

Taxes are one of the most confusing things for small business owners, especially those transitioning from the nine-to-five world. It's something that took me a very long time to figure out for myself, with a few errors along the way. I, unfortunately, paid the price my first couple of years in business by way of penalties for screwing up my taxes. It's still something that haunts me today!

Fortunately things have gotten easier over time. More and more good software exists (at bargain-basement prices) for taxes and record keeping, and going digital has been a really good way to be organized, efficient, and prompt with tax payments.

In this chapter, we'll approach this subject head-on. If you're like most people I know in the music industry, taxes are a difficult subject. In fact, some of my clients have never filed taxes, living somewhat off-the-grid when it comes to their finances as working musicians. But fear not—we'll work it out together. I know, I know, at this point you're probably saying, "But I just wanted to make music!" Don't worry—we've all said the same thing at some point, usually around mid-April.

When Should You Hire an Accountant?

Most people I know in the audio engineering world prefer to take on challenges head-on by themselves. I'm certainly one of those people, for better or worse. People like us can get quite bullheaded, especially when it comes to the finer points of running a business.

Unfortunately this can lead to some sticky situations, especially when it comes to your business expanding and the monumental differences in taxation situations. It's also hard to catch every single deduction that you're entitled to as well.

Hiring a tax professional shouldn't be a last resort; it should be part of your overall budget, if you plan to go anywhere past the small business phase. Remember, part of what makes your business successful is your drive and motivation, but also your expertise. Unless you came to the audio engineering world with a good background in finance, you will likely find that you need help. It's part of why this chapter is relatively short, compared to the vast amount of information and multiple complexities you can potentially encounter; only a trained tax professional can properly guide you and your unique situation.

Aside from good organizational skills and allowing you to free up your time and resources to better serve your clients, a good tax professional knows how to deal with the IRS. I remember the first time I ever got the dreaded white envelope requesting more information from my tax return—I had no idea what to do! Hiring a good tax professional will solve this problem for you before it becomes a much larger issue.

Taking Deductions

The first year I managed to do my taxes correctly (and all by myself, too!), I was really surprised at the number of legitimate business deductions I could take. As a small business owner, the tax code is certainly on your side when it comes to deducting expenses; that being said, you need to be careful, and above all, honest. The IRS can and will catch someone lying about the expenses they deduct. You may not think you're a potential target, but in the years I've worked with sole proprietors as clients, I can tell you—nobody's invisible to the IRS. The best way to deduct expenses is to do them honestly and within the guidelines of the law.

Among the expenses you can legally deduct from your recording studio business:

- The cost of necessary equipment for your studio (written off through the process of depreciation; more on this later), along with business supplies (paper, ink, etc.).
- Utility costs (Internet access, website hosting fees, electricity).
- Auto expenses for business vehicles, if you have any; for personal vehicles, you can deduct expenses paid on behalf of your business while using the personal vehicle, including mileage spent traveling on behalf of clients. You can choose, alternatively, to deduct actual expenses rather than mileage, if that number results in a more favorable deduction.

- Services rendered to your business (legal, handyman services, tax and accounting services).
- Half of your self-employment tax.
- Any travel or entertainment costs paid for business purposes.

Let's dig deeper into everybody's favorite part of doing their taxes—deductions. These laws were put in place to help you, so it's only fair you use them to your full advantage, right?

Deducting Your Home or Office Expenses

While it's certainly alright to use business income to pay the expenses of your rent or mortgage (you're a home-based business, after all), you can't deduct that full amount from your taxes, since only a portion of the home is used in business. Many studios expand to include a lot of space within the home—sometimes as much as 50 percent of the available space.

To fully understand the process of writing off a portion of your home and its expenses, you should check out *IRS Form 8829: Expenses for Business Use of Your Home*. This is a very helpful document, and it'll walk you through the process of deducting these expenses.

To find what percentage of your home is used for business, the IRS recommends the following formula:

- Find the area for the space you use. This is done by multiplying the length by the width of the room. For example: The area of my home studio space is 20 feet by 20 feet, for a total of 400 square feet.
- Divide the area by the total square footage of your home. My home is 1,200 square feet, so I use $1/3$ the available space for my studio.
- Thus, I use 33 percent of my home for business purposes, and I can deduct 33 percent of my housing expenses—including utilities, interest, and depreciation on the home itself.

Writing Off Equipment

As a business owner, one of the things you're able to do is write off the cost of equipment that you buy for your studio. This is great news—because as you are painfully aware, studio equipment isn't cheap. It's great to be able to recoup a portion of that investment through tax write-offs.

Writing off equipment is a lot easier than you'd think—under normal circumstances, you need to write it off over a period of time using a method known as depreciation. However, there's one piece of tax code that will come to your benefit, especially your first year in business when equipment expenses are really high.

According to the IRS Code, Section 179, if you purchase equipment that's used primarily in your business, you can deduct the full amount you paid from your gross income in the year you bought it. In 2010, that means you could write off up to $250,000 of equipment (including software) that you've purchased in that tax year. It's that easy—and it's a tremendous benefit to businesses buying lots of equipment, something recording studios do often.

The Section 179 deduction is something that you or your accountant will have to add to your tax return in addition to your normal paperwork. You'll need to fill out part 1 of IRS form 4562, and attach it to your tax return.

Deducting Start-Up Costs

As we talked about before, your business will have paid out potentially thousands of dollars in supplies before you've opened your doors. Keeping track of these start-up expenses is extremely important, because—you guessed it!—those can be written off, too.

The IRS generously allows you, in the year you start your business, to deduct up to $5,000 each per start-up expense (including consultancy fees, filing fees, and licenses), along with $5,000 of what's called *organizational costs*. Start-up expenses include things like advertising, consultant's fees, business plan research costs, and training costs.

Organizational costs are another thing that you'll be glad you can write off. Included in this category are your state and municipal licensing fees, legal fees for business structuring, and any filing fees associated with starting your business.

Keeping Good Records

One of the most painstaking things to remember, from day one, is to keep as accurate records as possible. This is one area in which people are usually either very, very good or very bad. There are extremes on either side, but it's always best to err on the side of caution when it comes to keeping information that is pertinent to your taxes.

We've been talking about dealing with creditors, and good recordkeeping is essential for this banking relationship. With good records from the very beginning, you'll be able to show detailed profit or loss statements showing how your business is doing. You should be able to account for every dollar coming in or going out of your business. Yes, it may seem intrusive, but that's what lenders these days require. Since the bottom fell out of the economy, you've got to compete and compete hard for every dollar lent. Having detailed records is a good start.

According to our friends at the IRS, keeping very good records is the first step to successfully managing your business's taxes, too (and, for that matter, your finances in general). There's a lot of different reasons you might need detailed records—depreciation, gain or loss of sold assets, and the dreaded tax audit. Among the records you should always endeavor to keep current:

- **Income statements, otherwise known as gross receipts.** Gross receipts are proof of the income you make through your business's activities. You should be able to generate a receipt for every client transaction that you make. The IRS will accept anything from credit card charge slips, bank deposit slips, printed invoices, 1099-MISC forms, receipt books, and handwritten receipts between you and a client. These documents show what monies came into the business, before expenses.

- **Business expenses.** Keep track of absolutely everything you spend in the name of the business; many things are deductible on your taxes later on, and if you plan to deduct, you'd better be prepared to be audited and to show proof that those deductions were legitimate. Here's one area where many small business owners screw up: Deductions are only legal if you have supporting proof. If you lose the receipt from an item bought for the business, account statements or credit card statements can also be used as supporting evidence. Canceled checks, cash register receipts, and invoices from merchants and suppliers all work to prove expenses, too.

- **List of assets.** The IRS likes to know about the expenses you've put out for your business, but they also need to know what you've got in your business's working space. This includes all of your recording equipment, furniture, office equipment, and anything else you use in the day-to-day operations of your business. To keep good asset lists, you'll need to document where and how you obtained the item; how much you paid for the item initially (and how much money you've put into repairs or improvements); depreciation deductions you take on your taxes; and, if the item has been sold or transferred, the conditions of the sale (donation, selling at a loss, sold at a profit, etc.).

Supporting Documents in the Digital Age

Believe it or not, it's not good enough to just write down income and expenses and call it a day. Good record keeping is about keeping yourself organized, but more importantly, out of trouble. Collecting supporting documents will take time, energy, and most importantly, space—that is, unless you go digital. Scanning your important documents—namely receipts, invoices, and payroll forms—can save you a lot of time, frustration, and space. Whether you go for the old documents-in-a-shoebox method or the more future-ready digital storage, there are a few things to remember about good record keeping.

There are many services that will scan documents and store them in safe, off-site backups for a reasonable monthly fee, but it's still something you can easily accomplish with a modestly priced scanner and some hard drive space. This allows you to easily index your documents, keep scans of them indefinitely, and be able to pull up any relevant paperwork from any point in time.

Other than sales receipts and paid invoices, you'll also want to archive any canceled checks and bank deposits. This is an easy one to understand—and something I didn't do in my business, which bit me later on. Let's say someone comes after you later and claims you didn't pay an invoice; having a canceled check as proof makes it all the easier to end the argument.

How Long Should You Keep Documents?

With the threat of an audit looming over every taxpayer's head (whether you're a likely candidate or not), it'll be to your benefit to store your documents long-term. That's why digital archiving is especially useful; you never know when you'll need to reference any of these important pieces of paper.

So how long should you plan to keep supporting documents for your small business?

- **Forever:** Financial records, tax returns, legal paperwork, tax checks, tax audit reports, business plans
- **Ten years:** Contracts, canceled checks, payroll records, accounts payable, and accounts receivable
- **Two to three years:** Banking paperwork (deposit slips, bank statements)

Other documents worth saving:

- **Detailed equipment inventory.** Make sure every piece of equipment is documented. Serial number, model number, and how much you paid for the item, including receipts showing exactly what you purchased it for, from whom, and when. These are useful for insurance purposes.
- **Proof of other deductible expenses.** Your business is able to write off many other expenses on your taxes, and you should make full use of this to the best of your ability. These include travel expenses, mileage expenses, lodging, meals, telephone calls for business, tips, taxi transportation, and many others.
- **Records of any monies paid on behalf of a client.** This includes gear rental, space rental, or any other expense you've had to incur due to a project, whether you billed this to the client or not. This may seem like a no-brainer, but if a client puts up a fight on reimbursing you, you need to be able to prove it.

Employer Identification Number

The IRS makes it rather easy to obtain an Employer Identification Number, or EIN, for small businesses. It's an online process that takes very little time and gives you a number for immediate use.

Why should you obtain an EIN? According to the IRS, you need an EIN if you're hiring employees, operating as a corporation or partnership, withholding any taxes on income, and a few other situations that are unlikely to apply to a recording studio. It's also a prerequisite for obtaining business credit, so it's a good idea to get one.

If you're operating as a sole proprietor, you don't need to provide your EIN on your tax returns—just file your taxes as normal. If you're filing as a corporation, you'll need that EIN.

Many online searches lead you to sites that offer to register your EIN for a fee. This is a shame, since the IRS makes it very easy to register for free online. Simply visit https://sa1.www4.irs.gov/modiein/individual/index.jsp and you'll receive your EIN instantly and free of charge.

Cash "Under The Table"

In a business like music, you'll run into a lot of people who don't do things "by the book." That's just a part of this industry that you'll have to learn to embrace. One of the most common situations for any self-employed person—is the cash payment. Cash payments are certainly convenient for both you and your client, as they don't automatically generate a paper trail and don't necessarily come up on the IRS's radar when passed "under the table." While it's certainly tempting to rely on under-the-table payments in cash—and thereby avoid taxes—take the safe way out: Account for every dollar that comes into your business, cash or not.

Accounting: Cash versus Accrual

One of the more important decisions in your business bookkeeping will be whether to go by the cash or accrual methods of accounting. Either way, you'll be accounting for everything that happens within your business, and by maintaining these bookkeeping efforts, you'll position yourself to be ready when tax season rolls around.

A good way to think of the two methods is this: Let's say you have a studio client who comes in to do some work in June. You perform the work and invoice the client. They pay your invoice in July. Using the accrual method, you would record this income as having been brought in during the month of June, because it was earned in June, not July—the cash from the job only became available to you in July. Using the cash method of accounting, you would show this income as having come when you actually received payment, in July.

The cash method of accounting is relatively easy, and it works almost identically to the way most of us take care of our personal finances. With cash accounting, you attempt to make a fairly real-time snapshot of your finances by only balancing income with deductions when they actually happen. It relies only on "real" data, meaning events that have already occurred. To use the cash method of accounting, you simply keep track of three things:

- **Cash on hand.** This would be the amount of money currently in your bank account (or held in cash).
- **Income, recorded when you receive the money.** A paid invoice from a client equals an increase in your cash balance for whatever time of the year it happens.
- **Expenses, deducted as you actually pay them.** Outstanding bills and invoices don't count against your overall financial picture; your balance only goes down when you actually pay the bill.

This is a very simple method of accounting, and the one that most small businesses use. It's certainly much easier if you're managing your business and personal finances in the same way, but one warning: This only shows your real-time cash balance, not your outstanding liabilities. You may look at your cash accounting snapshot and see a picture that's much brighter than reality—mainly because the costs associated with running the business may not have been deducted from the income yet.

With accrual accounting, the picture is a little more complicated—and potentially a much happier picture, though deceptively so. Accrual accounting is the method used by most larger businesses, who operate by extending credit to their customers, and who need to pay larger monthly expenses. It's also a method of accounting mainly useful for larger businesses operating with a large amount of cash in the bank, because it requires some careful planning and a reminder not to use the accrual method picture of your financial health in deciding when to spend money.

Accounting via the accrual method requires using two separate files, your *accounts receivable* file (where you keep track of the invoices you send to clients and when they pay them), as well as an *accounts payable* file (where you record bills and other expenses). Your accounts receivable file will keep track of all of the money you bring in, whether you've actually been paid for the services rendered yet or not.

To use the accrual method, you've got to do a couple of things differently than using the cash method:

- Document all services rendered (or income earned), even if the invoices are still outstanding, as income for the month you billed the services. For example, if you billed a client $35 for one hour of studio time to do some overdubs, your accounts receivable will show a $35 balance, even if they haven't paid you in full.
- List expenses when they occur, not as you pay them. When you pay the actual invoice is largely irrelevant, although you'll record this information, too.

As you can see, either method works well, depending on the structure of your business. But for most of the financial details of a small business like your recording studio, the cash method of accounting is superior, mainly due to its simplicity. True, it'll also take a keen understanding (and bookkeeping) of your outstanding liabilities and bills, but that's easy to accomplish with a little diligence and accurate bookkeeping.

Filing as Self-Employed

We've talked about the various ways you can be viewed by the government as a business—corporation, partnership, sole proprietor, etc.—and that can easily change how you file for your taxes.

As a newly self-employed person, chances are you'll be filing as a sole proprietor, which means you're self-employed. If you fall under this category, you must pay self-employment tax. Self-employment tax is a tax designed to make up for the Medicare and Social Security payments not being withheld from a regular nine-to-five paycheck. The first $106,800 of your income is subject to both 12.4 percent social security payments, and 2.9 percent Medicare tax as a self-employed person.

Don't forget your state income taxes, either—follow up with your state's income tax entity to determine how they'd like you to handle your state taxes.

If you had a tax liability the previous year, and expect at least $1,000 in tax payments for the upcoming year, you are also asked to pay estimated taxes. Estimated taxes are paid quarterly, and are based upon your liabilities for the previous year, along with your estimated liabilities, after credits, for the upcoming year. For your first year in business, it's up to you to figure out how much in taxes you feel you need to pay, based on your frequency of business and the income you're receiving. It's always smart to err on the side of caution and overpay your taxes; underpayment is subject to a penalty (and I speak from experience).

After your business has been open for a year, you'll have two options as to how you'll determine the amount of money to pay in taxes. First, you can use the previous year's tax return as your basis for paying the current year's tax; this is especially convenient because it doesn't require any complicated calculations to get a number that works. The downside is that if your business was successful (and you're making more money), you may end up with a tax deficit you'll have to pay.

Alternatively, you can take into account your previous year's earnings along with your projections for the current year, and use those to estimate 90 percent of your potential taxes, and pay those as you go. Either method works and both rely on you to be vigilant about your tax liabilities come tax return season.

08 Legal and Ethical Issues

Now that you've got your studio business off to a good start, it's time to look at some of the finer points of studio management. As we've been talking about all along, being a great engineer doesn't necessarily qualify you for running a successful studio. It's all about the details.

In this chapter we're going to take a look at two very important aspects of running a business: legal issues and ethical issues. As a business, you're going to be held to some very high standards by the law and by your clients. You'll need to be able to navigate the intricate legal and ethical web that comes along with not only business ownership, but the recording industry in general. Fortunately it's a lot easier than you might think. Despite what you might sometimes think, many local and state laws are designed to help small business rather than impede your success.

Let's look at some of the most important legal and ethical issues you'll run across while running your recording studio business.

Software Piracy

No matter what they might say when asked, almost everybody who's used a computer in the last few years has engaged in software piracy. Admittedly, I've done it, too—although in my professional studio today, all of my software is legal. Finding pirated software is relatively easy and, most importantly to most users, it's free. It's no secret, then, that many studios rely on software piracy to get the tools they feel they need. In fact, in some parts of the world, it's believed that somewhere between 80 and 90 percent of studios rely, at least partly, on pirated software to operate.

While software piracy may look like an easy (and cheap) way to have a full-featured recording setup, there are many reasons why you want to leave room in your budget to actually pay for the software you need.

Piracy is, first and foremost, illegal. Businesses that rely on pirated software are participating in an activity that could potentially cost thousands of dollars in fines and legal fees, not to mention downtime, if caught—and you'd be surprised how often this actually happens. Audits can occur remotely—some pirated apps can be encouraged to phone home and tattle on their users—or when a client comes into your studio and isn't happy that the project is being handled on a cracked, pirated version of a popular software. The legal penalties for software piracy vary with each municipality, but federally, the distribution and use of pirated software can potentially cost you up to five years in jail and a fine of up to $250,000.

Also, many times pirated software is cracked using methods that can make the software much less stable than retail versions. While the people who do software cracking are very talented programmers, they still make mistakes and make compromises to deliver a final product to the Internet. These methods will sometimes interrupt the natural workings of a software package when it hurts the most—sometimes while you're doing a deep edit or a long mix session. Legally purchased software—while still occasionally having hiccups due to your unique system profile—is generally free from such major issues.

The other issue is support. While most engineers will never admit it, most of us have had to call tech support at one time or another because something just wasn't materializing the way we wanted and we felt the software was the culprit. Pirated software doesn't allow you access to the industry-leading tech support that many of these companies offer. Half the time, Help files aren't even found bundled with pirated software—you're truly on your own. Using legitimately licensed software opens the doors to technical support and version updates, allowing you to stay current, especially with ever-evolving operating system updates that generally require software to follow suit to ensure compatibility. Most importantly, you'll be able to get help if something goes wrong during an important session; just think of the money you'll lose if you have a problem during a project and can't get things back up and running quickly.

There's also the moral angle of software piracy. Most audio software companies are relatively small operations, and some of the best are small home-based businesses just like yours. The licensing fees you pay help keep them in business providing support and updates for their software. It's not fair to these businesses to make a profit off of their product without paying your share to use them.

Before the Check Clears: Holding the Master

There's a popular joke in the studio community: "What's the stupidest thing I've ever done in my studio? Accepted a check." Yes, it's funny, but it's unfortunately true. Working with musicians, you've probably noticed that some of them, especially the most talented, somehow have this knack for being unprepared and unreliable. It's rare when you find somebody who's not only talented, but business savvy. Unfortunately that's the exception rather than the rule.

While most of your clients will, hopefully, be much too reliable to ever write you a bad check (or miss payments on services rendered), it's bound to happen eventually. This is another reason why comprehensive contracts are very important in this business—they keep you from being burned, and they give your client an incentive to do the right thing when it comes to finances, since they know that they're contractually bound.

That being said, one of the most important things to remember is to never let your client leave the studio with a usable copy of their material until you're paid in full. This includes digital rough mixes that you send out in MP3 format; those are just as good as a physical disk in today's world.

If your client wants to hear their progress, the best course of action is to allow them to hear everything they want in the comfort of your control room. Nothing— rough mixes, final mixes, or masters—should leave your hands unless you have every dollar you're owed. The reasoning is very simple: Even a rough mix sounds rather good with today's digital mixing software and is easily usable by the client. Yes, it's their material—you don't own the copyright just because they default on their payment—but you shouldn't let them have a usable product if they're not paid up. These rough mixes can easily be used for both digital and traditional physical distribution.

If you do decide to let your clients take material out of the studio, either by physical media or digital file, it's wise to watermark the files so they're not commercially useful. This can be easily accomplished in any two-track editor by inserting quick periods of noise or silence in the recording—I personally watermark all files with a burst of silence at 30-second intervals throughout the song. This will allow the client to listen to their work in their own surroundings, but prevent them from using the product further. No matter what, it's wise to request payment in full before the project begins, if your client can afford it.

Client Confidentiality and Project Security

Everyone's familiar with the term *leaked* in the music business. That's what happens when an album is released, for free, to the Internet before it's officially released for retail sale. This is a potentially damaging and traumatic incident for many bands, both major label and independent. Keeping your clients' projects safe and out of the wrong hands—assuming they're noteworthy enough to make their leaked album a commodity—is a very important part of your business.

I've had a client's work leak out before, and they weren't too happy about it. A few years ago, I mixed an acoustic studio session for a fairly well-known regional band; it sounded fantastic and they were very happy. They had scheduled the release date for sometime in the winter, and that fall I received a fairly angry call from the band's manager. He informed me that the band had found the album available on one of the BitTorrent sites that were popular at the time and demanded to know how it had happened. I scratched my head—the only people who had copies of the final product were the band, and they had accounted for all of their physical CDs. What possibly could have gone wrong?

Well, this one was my fault. I had downloaded a file sharing program, and at the time, I forgot to configure it only to work with a few select shared folders. Instead, my entire music library became openly accessible for a few days. In the meantime, someone did a search for the band, and since I had tagged the MP3s in iTunes, my session popped up on their search. The person had downloaded it from that folder and shared it among friends.

I immediately contacted the band and apologized—and they were very good sports about the whole thing. We even went on to record two more projects together since we meshed very well in the studio. Obviously I was lucky that time; if something similar happens to you, you may not be so lucky.

Now, when working with a client, I always take the following precautions to protect the security of their material:

- No digital files without watermarks, unless the client approves or requests otherwise (assuming they're paid up). It's very easy to forward on an MP3 or accidentally leave a directory shared on an Internet peer-to-peer network. True fact: My story aside, one major-label artist's album was leaked because they connected to the Internet peer-to-peer sharing site Kazaa, and a peeking fan found the directory shared. The label was not amused. Another popular band left a physical copy of a rough mix in a hotel room—and a cleaning crew member brought this home for a relative who was a big fan. While the Internet rejoiced as this fan leaked the album to the Internet, the band was really disappointed.

- Account for all physical copies. Whenever I give out rough mixes to clients who've paid for them, I number every piece of physical media and log who gets which disk number. I then ask for the rough mixes back at the beginning of each new session. This allows the demo disks to be accounted for, and any missing disks are easy to spot. Again, this assumes that the material is worth the effort for someone to pirate. Not every client, unfortunately, will be such a valued commodity.
- Shred all rough mix media. I use a simple, high-quality shredder that cost less than $50. After receiving rough mixes back, I shred them to avoid the copies falling into the wrong hands. Not only that, but it never hurts to eliminate useless media lying around the studio, because you should always want the highest-quality mixes floating around at hand.

While it's always a great idea to brag about your accomplishments for purposes of both pride and marketing, you should also make sure to respect your client's wishes in terms of confidentiality. Some clients, if they're high-profile for any reason, may wish to be excluded from your marketing efforts. That's fine, although many clients will allow you to at least list them on your website, even if they request that you not share what they worked on with you until after it's been released, which can sometimes take a while after the recording is done. Respect this, as breaking it would easily damage your reputation with quality clients, something no small business can afford.

Noise Pollution: Know (and Use) the Law

Noise, unfortunately, is a recording studio's biggest downfall. You're in the business of making noise for a living and while it's second nature to folks like you and me, your neighbors might not feel the same way. I've seen a lot of good studios fall victim to misunderstandings with neighbors, and for this reason, understanding the noise laws in your municipality can help greatly.

While the local laws are too numerous to possibly list here, take some time to find out your local noise ordinances. Calling your local police station is the first step, as they're generally very willing to help a small business stay on the good side of the law (and their neighbors).

Many noise pollution issues can be solved (or at least kept from becoming major issues) by doing three things:

1. **Select your recording space wisely.** We talked about this early on, but if you're in a communal living situation (apartment, condo, etc.), you've got some really important decisions to make. Running a business of any type where clients will be coming and going at all hours typically doesn't go over very well with some types of neighbors, but noise is a general complaint that everybody can relate to. Make sure that your recording space is in a location that won't cause anybody else noise problems at bad times.

2. **Watch the hours you operate.** While your neighbors may not appreciate your noise, they'll certainly appreciate you if you make an effort to work out the issues with them ahead of time. Sitting down with your neighbors, explaining your business, and being kind, understanding, and patient when they express their concerns will go a long way. You'll also be able to work with them to set hours for certain activities—for example, you can only track live drums until 8:00 p.m. at night—that keeps everybody happy.

3. **Know the law.** We talked about this briefly, but knowing your local ordinances will keep you running if things get ugly with the neighbors. If your neighbors have failed to reach a compromise with you, default to the law of your city, which might say that noise can't reach a certain decibel level or that noise must be done at a certain hour of night. Keeping your studio operations within this law—and always keeping in touch with your local law enforcement and their policies to avoid problems—will help you.

Drugs and Alcohol in Your Studio

I've worked with a lot of different clients over the years, and most of them were extremely professional and pleasant people to work with. Some weren't—and a lot of that had to do with the vices they chose to indulge themselves in while working with me in the studio. I wasn't around to see the glory days of rock 'n' roll excess within the industry, but I've heard stories—and I occasionally work with relics from that age who still party like it's part of their job.

While the old saying "sex, drugs, and rock 'n' roll" has gone on to become the battle cry of the music industry, it's from a different time. Labels today are running much leaner operations, and artists simply aren't getting paid what they used to. In fact, you'd be surprised at the personal lives of some very popular bands—some good friends of mine, musicians who've earned a lot of great success in their respective music careers, would be mistaken for just any other suburban, taxpaying citizen if viewed from the outside. The image of what constitutes a rock star has certainly changed with the times.

While the hard-partying ways of eighties hair bands may be gone, it's no secret that musicians come in varying types, from the conservative, straight-edge bands to hard partiers that would make Spinal Tap blush—I've worked with both types and everything in between.

When bands come into the studio, some of them view it as an excuse to party. They want the studio experience to mimic that of their rock star heroes—and that's not always something you should allow. That being said, many bands will appear to be very professional and take working in the studio extremely seriously.

Whether to allow alcohol use in your studio is up to you. Many studios will allow clients to bring in whatever they wish, as it usually aids in comfort and creativity. It's perfectly legal, too, as long as everybody involved is over twenty-one years old. Allowing extreme intoxication is not smart, for logistical and safety reasons. You've got a lot of liability by having intoxicated people in your place of business—drunk individuals can easily injure themselves or somebody else and cause serious damage to property.

As far as money goes, when you're charging by the hour, there's no time to waste with someone who's too drunk to work, and the band isn't paying you to host their drinking party. It should be made very clear in your preproduction meetings with your clients what your expectations are when it comes to behavior in your studio.

Drugs, however, should never be allowed. While many musicians enjoy smoking marijuana for both creative and relaxation purposes, allowing an illegal item into your place of business is never a smart move, even something as relatively harmless as a few joints. Hard drugs, on the other hand, should be dealt with swiftly. You want to make sure that you're not involved in anything that can cast a potential shadow on your business, and drugs are one of those things. I've kicked bands out of my studio for bringing drugs, and others have asked what my policy is up front. While it's ultimately your call—it's your business, after all—allowing something as blatantly illegal as drugs can be a show-stopper under the wrong circumstances. All it takes is an officer responding to a routine noise call to your studio, and everybody's day gets a lot longer. No matter your personal feelings about the issue, it's still illegal to possess and use drugs.

Equipment Theft

Studios are expensive to stock, as you've undoubtedly found out by now. Microphones, outboard equipment, audio interfaces, and cabling can quickly add up. Whether you've spent $1,000 or $30,000, whatever equipment you have in your studio is your biggest asset, outside of your engineering skills. Protecting this equipment from theft is extremely important and relatively cheap.

While a robbery is the most likely way you'll lose gear, don't look past a client or their guests stealing something from your studio. You've got a lot of valuable gear, especially small items that can easily walk off—microphones, for example. While I've luckily never had my studio robbed, I have had items stolen by clients. Here are a few tips to help you avoid theft at your studio:

- **Keep quality inventory.** Make sure everything—from microphones to pre-amps to mixers to USB drives—is accounted for. Documenting these items in a spreadsheet is just fine. Keep track of serial numbers, the appearance of each item, and its function. If something goes missing, this information will help you greatly.
- **Engrave what you can.** Microphones—the good ones, anyway—are usually made of a hard metal which is suitable for engraving. It can be simple: your initials or a serial number in an inconspicuous place. Labeling in this way really helps with locating your gear later on if it disappears. I've had fellow engineers reclaim expensive, long-lost stolen microphones by being able to explain engravings.
- **Insurance, insurance, insurance.** I can't say this one enough: Make sure your gear is insured, and make sure your policy covers actual replacement cost, not a prorated time-sensitive valuation of the item. Being able to file a claim, pick up a new piece of equipment, and continue where the session left off is a big advantage. Yes, good insurance costs money—but so does downtime during an expensive project. I'll take $50 per month over thousands of dollars of lost revenue any day.

Recording Cover Songs

Artists love recording cover songs. In fact, many bands make a great living only playing cover tunes. Sometimes these artists make incredible salaries compared to original, independent musicians (I'll spare you my feelings on that disparity), because parties and corporate gigs pay huge amounts of money for danceable, familiar music presented with the energy of a live performance. Unfortunately, recording cover songs—as profitable as it may be for the artist and thereby your business—comes with a little bit of legal negotiation that needs to take place first. Helping your clients navigate this intricate web of legal matters will greatly benefit both you and your client, and keep you both out of the crosshairs should the copyright holder be unhappy with the cover song being recorded. This applies only to songs which are held in copyright by an artist; many songs are considered public domain and can be freely covered without mechanical licensing.

This being said, your client may already have a standing agreement with an artist to cover a song, on either a royalty-free or reduced-royalty basis. These types of agreements are indeed common, but should be in place before recording begins.

First of all, keep in mind that covering a song isn't necessarily stealing. Stealing a song—and thus creating true copyright infringement—is when your client records a significant portion of an already existing piece of intellectual property without credit and licensing to the original artist. Recording a cover song is a somewhat complicated affair, and thanks to the Copyright Act of 1909, recording artists have the legal ability to record a cover version of any song they like, with or without the express written permission of the copyright holder.

This type of licensing is called a *compulsory license*, which grants what's called either a *mechanical license* or *digital license*. Mechanical licenses:

- Allow the sale of copyrighted works through physical media
- Allow permanent digital download, which includes sale on iTunes Music Store or other digital outlets where the consumer buys the song and keeps the digital file

In comparison, digital licenses grant the recording artist the rights to:

- Sell the cover song as a ring tone
- Allow limited-time downloads, where the user is essentially renting the material

- Allow streaming services to use the cover version on their services, as a feature to paid subscribers

Under a standard compulsory license, the artist recording the cover song adheres to a few guidelines in order to be granted a mechanical license. The recording artist must:

- Notify the copyright holder, in writing, thirty days before the planned distribution of the recording; this type of letter is called a "Compulsory License Letter."
- Pay a mechanical licensing fee, which is essentially an advance royalty paid to the publisher of record for the artist who originally wrote the song. This is paid in advance for the number of units to be initially sold.
- Continue to pay future royalties on a recurring basis along with accounting of units sold after the initial run.
- Include individual writer and publisher credit listings in the materials sold with each physical copy. For digital copies, the writing and publishing information must be included on the data accompanying the file itself.

Until December 31, 2012, the mandatory rates that a recording artist must pay to cover and release a song are as follows:

- For physical sales, 9.1 cents for up to five minutes in length; 1.75 cents for each minute over five, rounded up.
- For permanent digital downloads, the same fee structure applies.
- For ringtones, 24 cents per unit.

For permission to stream songs through nonpermanent digital music distributors (such as Pandora, Rhapsody, and satellite radio), you'll need to negotiate directly with the copyright holder, depending on what services the recording will be used by. The cost varies, from 15 cents to 30 cents per subscriber, depending on the type of service and other legal variables. The good news is that many of these services negotiate with the copyright holders and pay a bulk rate ahead of time.

So how does your client obtain this compulsory license and pay the required publishing fees?

- Locate the copyright holder. The Harry Fox Agency (www.harryfox.com) is one of the largest publishing royalty licensing companies. Many artists allow licenses to be purchased directly online.

- If the copyright holder can't be dealt with through The Harry Fox Agency, you'll need to reach out directly. Services like ASCAP and BMI offer online listings of publishers and copyright holders. With that information you can write a Compulsory License Letter to the copyright holder. This will initiate a dialogue between the parties, allowing for the rate to be paid properly. The copyright holder may request a copy of the material as well.
- Pay the required fees per unit sold. The Harry Fox Agency asks you to pay these up front; if you're dealing with the publisher directly, you can usually pay per unit as they're sold, with monthly statements of sales. These can, of course, be negotiated if you go directly to the publisher and ask politely; don't count on this to happen if your client is a small player in the game, where the royalties, even at the full rate, won't make much money for the publisher.

Though the likelihood of a small, independent band like many of your clients getting in trouble for recording a cover song without going through the proper steps is rather minimal, it's still a good idea to always follow the rules. Encourage your client to stay on the proper side of the law.

There's one exception to this process that your clients should be aware of. With the advent of digital file sharing and the easy accessibility of demos, rough mixes, and live recordings, your client should make sure that the song they're recording has already been released by the artist who wrote it. The one exception to compulsory mechanical licensing is if the song hasn't officially been released yet—in that case, the original copyright holder has the ability to deny a mechanical license to the requester until the song is first released officially by the artist themselves. This is only fair—an artist who has a really good song and hasn't released it yet should be entitled to release it first, even if your clients have recorded what they consider the definitive version!

Generic Records & Distributors

Publishing Division

2165 Sample Place

Detroit, MI 48201

Notice of Intention to Obtain a Compulsory License for Making and Distributing Phonorecords

To Whom It May Concern:

The band *SAMPLE BAND* hereby notifies your company of their intent to record and distribute a song administered by your organization under a standard compulsory license as allowed by US Copyright law.

Legal Name: Shawn Smith and Robert Jones, d/b/a *SAMPLE BAND* Song: Epic Song

Author: Eric Jackson

Expected Configuration: Digital Phonorecord Delivery

Length of Recording: 4 minutes, 13 seconds

Expected First Date of Distribution: October 25, 2011

Name of Band Performing: *SAMPLE BAND* As required and expected, a statement of account under the compulsory license will be sent once a month on or before the 20th of every month, unless another arrangement is acceptable or more convenient, along with the required royalty payment at a rate of 9.1 cents per copy sold or distributed.

Sincerely,

Sample Band Representative

09

Marketing Your Studio

Being a really good audio engineer and stocking up on the latest and greatest gadgets is just the first step to running a successful recording studio. Unfortunately, the phrase "build it and they will come" wasn't exactly coined with budding businesses in mind.

Now that you've got your operations off the ground, it's time to start marketing your studio. Advertising is a key part of any business—but especially one that's new, like yours. Many established studios get by solely on word-of-mouth referrals between clients, and the consistent standard of quality that they put forth time after time. Unfortunately you're a brand-new business. Even with an impressive demo reel from freelance work, clients won't come based on your technical merits alone; first you'll need to be able to prove your studio can work well with clients to produce stellar results.

Until then, it's all about marketing. But lucky you! You're starting a business at one of the easiest times to get free or discounted promotion, with the Internet and social networking at your disposal.

Being a recording studio offers a unique set of challenges in terms of advertising. It's the same deal as a restaurant or any other service-based business—you're only as good as your last client served. You'll have to build your studio's reputation as a facility, but also spend time promoting yourself as an engineer. It's all about networking, getting your name out there, and letting the right customers know you've got a great product.

Marketing as a New Business

Businesses live and die because of clients, or the lack thereof. As a new business, you're in a challenging situation. How do you convince your clients that you're worth their time and money if they've never heard of you?

Getting your name out there doesn't have to be expensive. As we've talked about before, the digital age has made small business marketing a lot more accessible and very affordable for those of even the most modest means.

As a small business, you've got to look at your competition before planning your marketing strategy. We've talked about remaining competitive with the big guys in your local scene, but let's take a look at the big picture—including your smaller competition.

- What does your studio have to offer that the others don't? It could be that you're the highest-quality studio in town, or the coziest, smallest operation best suited for indie singer/songwriters. Either way, play up your strengths.
- Are you positioned to service clients of all means? Before aggressively marketing your business, consider your target markets. Offering a set of products that appeals to high-end clientele and one that's within reach of independent, budget-conscious clients allows you to service both equally—and there's always room for those low-end customers to evolve into higher-paying ones.
- Plan your advertising carefully. As a new business, your advertising budget will be secondary to the budget you've set for other, more pressing aspects of the business, such as equipment, licensing, and setting up your business's physical presence. Taking the time to learn your market is one of the most important things you can do for your budget.

All about Exposure

As long as you're offering a good product—and the feedback from your clients has been good enough to tell you this—it's time for you to use your successful projects for some exposure. They say any exposure is good exposure—and for a budding business, that's very true. Getting your name out there in any positive way is always a plus, and any chance you have to expose your business to potential clients will help your cause tremendously.

Just be aware that there is such a thing as too much exposure. You've got to be careful that you don't overdo it to the point of becoming a nuisance. In today's world of social networking and message boards, the music community—and audio engineering community, especially—is a lot smaller than you might think, especially in your local scene. You don't want to get yourself into a situation where you're viewed as spamming your services—in today's digital world, that's an instant way to lose business.

Go for the Ears First!

In chapter 4, we talked about putting together a demo reel, as an engineer. It's absolutely essential to do this as your studio opens; it's even more important to maintain it as time goes on. As an audio engineer, your job is to make things sound good, right? Most clients you work with really do care about the equipment you're using—they'll get as excited about ribbon microphones and tube compressors as you do. But many clients, even the gearheads, will appreciate what they hear more than what they see. This is where being a smaller, home-based studio really has its advantages. You're in a great position to truly excite the listener with your work— even if it's on more modest gear in a smaller setup than most larger commercial studios. Your skill as an engineer becomes the most valuable commodity of the business. Show that you can work magic despite dealing with limited resources.

So what standards should you always make sure to feature in your work to ensure commercial appeal?

1. What are the dominant music scenesters doing? Is it hip-hop or alt country? If you're able to show proficiency with making the local sound your own, you'll go far with many of your clients. Don't box yourself in, though— unless specializing is your ultimate goal (and the local scene offers enough clients that it makes financial sense)—you shouldn't limit yourself to one type of sound over another.
2. Study what the national music scene is doing production-wise. Are you able to Auto-Tune vocals and heavily process drums? If not, then you might not be viewed as current enough for pop/rock clients.
3. Make sure you're ready for the digital revolution. This means loud, punchy mixes suitable for being heard on today's consumer electronics. This doesn't mean you have to sacrifice your personal views about competing in the volume wars—just make sure your material sounds the best for the playback medium it will most likely be heard on and where your clients will likely evaluate your work.

You, As a Brand

Even with a room of high-quality gear, your engineering skills are arguably the most important thing you can possibly market. If it weren't for the fact that you have good skills, you wouldn't have even entertained the idea of opening a recording studio, and it's your skills that will get you through your projects and win over your clients' hearts. While it may seem like overkill, you should view your business as two separate entities: you, the engineer and producer; and your recording studio, the equipment and space that makes the magic happen.

Part of building this brand is to promote yourself and your accomplishments. Websites like LinkedIn, Facebook, and MySpace allow you to build your profile as an audio engineer. Publishing your résumé and demo reel—even if it includes work done outside your studio—is extremely important.

It might seem like you're feeding your ego, but in this case, it's alright—as long as you don't become obnoxious about it. People who are considering trusting you with their material (and their money) want to know they're in good hands. In fact, many artists live by the common industry mantra, "Choose your engineer, then your studio." So what can you do to help promote yourself as a good engineer?

- Don't be afraid to put your name out there in any way you can. If you've got good writing skills, offer to be a guest writer on popular blogs and websites. There's never a shortage of demand for experts who can clearly explain technical details to a nontechnical audience and gearheads alike. Any chance to show yourself as an expert in your field is always looked at by potential clients as a bonus.

- Subscribe to a reporter-source mailing list, such as Peter Shankman's Help A Reporter Out (HARO). HARO is a great free resource that allows experts to browse thrice-daily e-mail postings seeking experts to comment in major media outlets. This is a great way to get exposure in your field; as a quoted expert on music production and entertainment industry issues, you'll quickly develop a reputation for being top in your field. This can't hurt business, either. To subscribe, visit www.helpareporter.com.

- Participate in message boards and online forums. Interfacing with other engineers as well as working musicians is always a great way to boost your presence in the scene. While these forums don't offer the mass-media exposure of being quoted by or writing for media outlets, there's a level of credibility that comes from interacting in a civil and educated manner with others in your field. Offering advice, criticism, and support to entertainers and engineers alike provides more positive exposure.

Establishing a presence for yourself via the Internet is extremely important, because it allows you to have a personal connection to past and potential future clients. You know the old saying, "Out of sight, out of mind?" It doesn't only apply to overdue bills and dirty dishes—it also applies to you, and to anyone else who needs to maintain a good reputation for their services and skills among clients.

Social Networking

The Internet has come such a long way in just a few years, and it's been an especially great development for independent musicians. The new digital revolution is credited for the surge in successful independent music, and many artists that would have remained largely obscure five to ten years ago can find great success by employing social media to their advantage. The same holds true for recording studios and audio engineers.

Today, bands have been signed exclusively due to their YouTube videos, and independent artists are able to achieve unheard of sales records due to their own magnificent digital hustling. Advertising through social networking is free and offers a way to directly connect with your potential clients. It's something that bands twenty or thirty years ago could only dream of as they worked their tails off to sell cassettes from the trunk of their car post-gig.

Remember, many metro areas have relatively small and contented music communities. Even a large city may have a few key groups of players, and getting in good with one of these groups may give you access to not only new customers, but repeat business. Social networking makes it very easy for you maintain these relationships, which will greatly help your cause.

Facebook and (to a lesser extent) MySpace are considered the top leaders in social networking, especially in music-related categories. Establishing a profile for your business on these sites allows you to easily network with musicians—offering words of support and encouragement, and potentially keeping you in their thoughts when they decide to record.

Let's look at a few key factors that make up a really successful profile for a recording studio business on these popular social-networking sites.

- **Offer information but don't go overboard.** Make sure your potential clients know who you are, what services you offer, and a select list of past clientele. Don't go into long rants about rates, policies, and procedures. This isn't the time for business negotiations.
- **Post photographs of what you do best**—mixing, recording, and working with your clients. Your business profile isn't a place for personal photos. Your potential clients won't appreciate having to wade through copious amounts of personal garbage to learn more about your business. Just because you got your picture taken next to scantily-clad promotional models at a music industry convention doesn't mean you should post it on your studio's Facebook page.
- **Keep an up-to-date demo reel available through the site.** Signing up on these sites as a musician or band allows you to showcase your audio work. Obtain permission from select clients to use some of their material as clips on these sites. This is very important—perhaps the most important part of all!
- **When writing your profile, don't hype.** Write well and write clearly. Don't sell yourself as something you're not, and don't be unprofessional—that includes obscenities and talking badly about competitors or past clients.
- **Be active, be accessible.** Encourage potential clients to write you and have a dialogue about their needs, and frequently update your profile so as to appear interested and engaged in the online world. While it may not seem like much, seeing that someone last logged into their profile six months ago shows me they're not serious about promoting their image or business.

When deciding who to "friend" on a social-networking site, don't spam. Many companies offer friend-adding services to help businesses and bands with their promotions, but don't fall into this trap. What you're essentially paying for is someone to electronically harvest profile links from users' pages and send friend requests by the hundreds (or thousands) on behalf of your business. While friending strangers—and offering a personal introduction—can certainly help business, doing so on such a mass scale is downright irresponsible, not to mention tacky. This works on the principle that after so many blind friend requests, a percentage are bound to add you. All this does is increase your numbers, not necessarily your useful impressions on potential clients. You also don't want to be seen in the eyes of serious prospective clients as someone who has to so blindly reach for friends.

Working for Free

Many times creative professionals—recording studios included—are asked to work on "spec"—that's a fancy way of saying, you do the work and the client pays only if they like it. I'm sure you can see why this is a problem. You're not guaranteed a dime for your time and effort. Further, the potential client can take the ideas and practical applications you've come up with and use them on their own, essentially stealing your production input.

That being said, sometimes the opportunity will arise for you to take on a pro bono project, either for a commercial client or a nonprofit enterprise. Sometimes doing this type of work—provided it doesn't interfere with paying clients or prevent you from turning a freebie into a paid venture—can help your exposure and thus act as free advertising.

I ask myself the following questions before taking on a charity case:

- Does the project require more than five hours of my time to complete and is it within a reasonable deadline?
- Is there a reasonable chance the client can make a large financial profit from the work?
- Will the free project cost me anything other than time? If taking on a charity project necessitates the use of subcontracted equipment or space, it's not wise to go into the red for a project that's not paying you—or, you could offer to split the difference. If the freebie client pays for the accessory costs of the project, your time and services will be free.

While freebies are best used for organized nonprofit clients, musicians can be deep charity cases themselves. Working musicians are interesting people to work with—generally easygoing and very passionate about their art. They're also very dedicated to their music, many times to the point of putting music before gainful employment. This, of course, means that many working musicians are forced into a certain type of Do-It-Yourself culture, which makes your services not a necessary part of their budget. Take this as a challenge: If you gamble some time and energy, you may make longstanding connections with potentially successful (and thus paying) clients by offering some reduced-rate or free services to them in their currently cash-strapped state.

I'm not advocating taking on charity cases as a rule—especially with the large number of desperate musicians—but a few well-placed freebies for a band or two

Giving away free product is a time-honored tradition in helping a company promote its services. No matter what, free product still costs you in time and resources. If a good project comes along, here's a worksheet to figure out how much it'll really cost you to give a client a freebie.

How many billable hours will the project take to complete? _____

_____

_____

_____

How would you normally bill this project (flat rate or hourly)? _____

_____

_____

_____

What amount of paid business will you lose by prioritizing this project? _____

_____

_____

_____

What is this client's potential for repeat business? _____

_____

_____

_____

Can you afford to not make any money during the course of this project taking up your resources? _____

_____

_____

_____

with an extremely promising future but without a dime to their name can do wonders. It's free advertising, and it's always possible that these clients will remember you when they're in a position to become a paying client.

I don't recommend doing this for profit-seeking corporate clients, though. Even the most well-meaning corporate client still has a bottom line to look after, and your working for free to help someone else make a profit isn't a good idea. Bands are generally not organized into business structures until well into their career; bands are also not likely to be profit-making enterprises until a long time into their career (you'd be surprised how many major label bands aren't turning a profit). More often than not, working your way into a band's inner circle by way of a few generous endeavors can endear you to them for the remainder of their career. Sometimes, that's way better than what any advertising can do!

10

The Internet and E-Commerce

We've been talking a lot about leveraging the Internet to advertise your business. Being engaged with your online audience is absolutely necessary in today's digital world. Potential clients are plentiful and they're all online, waiting to be found. Past clients, as well, can be easily kept in the loop via social networking. But how else can you make the best use of the digital revolution for your business?

As anyone who's ever used the Internet for advertising can tell you, Internet advertising rates have plummeted. Paid advertising agencies now have to compete with free advertising avenues such as Craigslist and Backpage that offer businesses the chance to reach clients free of charge; they've also got to compete against the overwhelmingly popular social media sites where you're also advertising without cost. This is great for you as a new business on a budget!

Let's look at a few channels you can use to harness the Internet's full marketing power.

Your Website

In today's world of social networking, many businesses forego a website completely. Websites cost money to design, set up, and maintain. For some businesses, it might make sense to keep your Internet reach centered around social networking. For studios, however, maintaining a thorough and detailed website is equally important—even with the added costs involved.

When designing a website for your studio business, there're a few things you need to include in order to give potential clients the most accurate picture of what they can expect when working with you. These include:

- **Downloadable (or better yet, streaming) portfolio.** This allows you to showcase samples of work from prominent clients and projects. Did you take an unpolished band and make them sound incredible? Upload it. Here's your chance to show off your skills. Musicians will love hearing what you did with other bands, especially if they can picture themselves getting a similar treatment.

- **Photos of your space.** You'll want to show off your recording space to assure your clients that you're prepared for their projects. Many musicians know that the basics—a good live room and good isolation room—make all the difference, and they'll be looking to make sure you can offer them an advantage over recording in their bedrooms. Seeing a well-organized, professional-looking studio does wonders to give your clients extra reassurance that they'll be in good hands.
- **An accurate gear list.** If you've got some excellent backline gear or instruments, show them off! Proud of your collection of preamps and microphones? Show them off. Your clients are probably gearheads just like you. They'll really love to hear about your API EQs and your Neve clone preamps, just as you like telling everyone about them. Thinking about the fun gear they'll get to work with always entices musicians.

We talked about this before, but here's where your demo reel becomes extremely important. It's the way your clients will check out your work and decide if you're who they're looking for when it comes time to record an album. Most demo reels on social-networking sites consist of highly compressed, custom-encoded audio files that don't sound the best. They're designed with high efficiency in mind, costing the social-networking company very little to host and stream. This doesn't always offer the best representation of your quality work, so hosting your own demo reel online—where you're able to set the quality of audio files however you like—is a distinct advantage.

To prepare audio for your website's demo reel, you should first check with your chosen web designer (or decide for yourself, whichever way you choose to go) on how the audio files will be streamed through your website. Then, directly from your master recordings, you should encode them in the highest bit rate possible for sharing on your website; this could be high-resolution MP3 files, uncompressed WAV files, or lossless-compression FLAC files (the latter two options being perfect if you choose to offer your reel for download, as opposed to streaming-on-demand).

Depending on who you choose to design your online presence, you should expect to spend anywhere between a hundred and a couple thousand dollars on a very well-executed website. The least expensive options involve simple, modest online presences with little in the way of multimedia. The most expensive ones use Adobe Flash and other interactive elements to create an all-encompassing user experience. If you've got the added budget to pay for a website, it's an investment worth making since virtually everybody has access to the web. That being said, if it's not something you can comfortably pay for, a web presence via social networking is usually enough for most start-up businesses.

Digital Delivery

Another important thing to think about when planning your Internet presence is how you'll handle online product delivery. Many clients will prefer being able to receive their work digitally, instead of dealing with physical media. As an audio engineer, chances are you're familiar with the formats required for efficient, lossless, high-quality audio file delivery, namely FLAC and SHN compression.

The easiest way to do this is to partner with an excellent web-hosting service. You'll be able to get more than enough space to host your website along with a few gigs worth of space for some private file hosting. These files must be able to be secured by password, as your clients' files have to be held highly confidential for both commercial and personal reasons.

When choosing your service provider, make sure they don't charge you an arm and a leg if you need to add more space. Also, make sure there's no added charge for data transfers over a certain gigabyte. You might end up paying a great deal of money for these extra fees if you don't plan ahead; transfer fees add up very fast.

Craigslist

One of the most interesting and useful resources for those in the creative field is Craigslist. Craigslist is a simple, free message board and online classifieds site, with many sites tailored to individual locations. For a full list, see www.craigslist.org. If you've got a local Craigslist site, make use of it! Posting in the Musicians and Music Instruments categories is always a great way to meet potential clients. And it's not just posting advertisements for your services: Interacting with the local musicians gives you an opportunity to offer advice, show off your expertise, and build yourself up as a member of the music community.

Craigslist is ideal for most budding businesses because of the price tag: It's free. It's also localized, so you're not taking a stab in the dark trying to pull in local clients on sites with a broader reach. Many studios find success using free ads on Craigslist, but be careful not to spam too much. Members of these forums are generally vigilant about calling out those who use too much space for frequent advertisements.

Paying for Internet Advertising: Is It Worth It?

It may seem redundant to actually pay for Internet advertising; with so many free options out there, including social-networking sites and Craigslist, paying for Internet advertising for your studio may not be something you feel is necessary. While leveraging the Internet's exposure is one of the best things you can possibly do for a budding business, paying for it might not be in the budget right away. That's alright.

Internet advertising services do one thing, and do one thing well: Drive traffic to your website, where your potential customers will determine if they'd like to hire you. That's why a website (or linkable social-networking profile) is key when using one of these services. However, given the social nature of the music industry, these services may not be worth the money.

To put it into perspective, think where you'll likely find most of your clients. While many studios have great success using services such as Google Adwords, where you set your own budget and only pay for the amount of clicks you can afford, many other paid advertising schemes don't work quite as well for this type of business. Your biggest reach will come from social networking and advertising via community-based sites such as Craigslist and Backpage. As your client base expands and you feel like you need to reach a larger audience, paying for services such as the aforementioned Adwords becomes not such a bad investment.

Forums

A lot of audio engineers have found success in meeting new clients via networking in online forums. There are millions of Internet forums on every subject imaginable, and as you probably know already, there are several great ones devoted to everything involved with music and audio. Meeting other engineers is about a lot more than sharing tips about mixing and mastering—it's about getting in touch with your peers and being in a position to share work. You never know when you may need to find an engineer to subcontract out some work.

Advertising without paying for ad space on forums can be a risky endeavor. Most forums are advertiser-supported, so they frown upon free advertisements that don't necessarily benefit the community. Some will allow it—be careful to read the forum's instructions and rules, and contact a moderator if necessary. You certainly don't want to go from valued contributing member to spammer simply because you broke the rules of forum etiquette.

That being said, many forums will welcome your contributions as a member of the trade. You'll be able to easily network, show off your skills, and perhaps bring in some business for yourself. Being active with potential clients (and fellow engineers) shows that you are an audio engineer who is up-to-date on current trends, cares about standards in the industry, and wants to have a full online presence.

11 Training and Certification

How well do you know your chosen vocation of audio engineering? Even though I've been working with audio for over ten years, I'm always surprised at the things I still learn. We've got the privilege of working in one of the most dynamically changing industries—just think of how far we've come in the last five years—and as engineers, we owe it to ourselves and our clients to stay up to date on the latest trends in all aspects of our jobs.

Fortunately, keeping up to date in our industry is very easy. There are a lot of great resources for continued education in all areas of audio engineering, and many of them are actually fairly inexpensive (or free). With such a constantly changing industry, it's always necessary to stay informed of current trends to keep your clients coming back to you.

Staying Relevant

One of the worst things an audio engineer can do, especially one who owns a recording studio, is get behind the times. I know of a handful of engineers who've lost business because their operations became dated and expensive to maintain; other engineers have been stubborn about changing their way of recording and mixing because they're more comfortable with dated, analog-type approaches. While it's not always a problem to stick to the technology you know best, just as with many other service-industry businesses your clients will expect you to be ahead of the curve. It will take a lot more than just having the best gear to play with to keep your clients happy. In the past few years, the revolution of high-quality digital gear has allowed many studios to not only save their clients many thousands of dollars by operating sessions more quickly and efficiently, but the quality-for-cost ratio has swung in favor of many lower-budget operations because the better gear available for a lower price has opened up many options previously reserved for the higher-dollar studios.

But equipment aside, what can you as an engineer do to keep yourself ahead of the game? First of all, and most importantly, keeping up with your peers in the audio recording industry will help you stay informed with trends and developments that will make your job easier (and a lot more fun). Networking with others also creates opportunities to pick up business when others can't take it. I can't tell you how many times a session was saved because I had the right people to call when a client needed something outside of my general scope of knowledge.

Don't assume that just because you know how to record, mix, and work the politics of the music industry you're at the top of your game. You'll save yourself a lot of frustration and buy yourself way more business, if you keep on top of current technological and aesthetic trends within the recording industry.

How Client Expectations Change

Over the years, recording in smaller studios—especially home-based businesses—has been a risky proposition for professional musicians. Without certain amenities, clients sometimes wonder if they are getting a quality product. Remember my story about one of my first clients? He was disappointed not by the product my studio could produce—in fact, he loved some of the clips I sent him early on in our discussions—but he couldn't get past the fact that the encyclopedic image of a recording studio in his head didn't match what he was seeing in my modest home studio. Those preconceived notions have, for the most part, been forgotten as more and more artists understand the recording studio of the digital age. Times have changed greatly, and as we've talked about quite a bit, there's a lot of exceptional work coming out of home-based studios.

In the last few years, there's been a large shift in the quality attainable for lower prices and your clients' expectations will also follow suit. As your studio evolves, you'll find that your clients tend to expect more of you, even if they're not paying more. Working musicians now have access to small home-based recording equipment which can give them decent results without an ongoing investment, so you'll need to start offering a lot more than the basics in order to compete with their own recording efforts.

So how can you keep ahead of the pack? When it comes to industry-standard features that today's clients expect, here's a list to keep in mind when building your studio. In fact, I'm always finding clients who call me and ask me about some of these key features first, well before we've ever actually discussed their project. And as sad as it is, saying "Yes, I have Auto-Tune!" has won me more business than saying, "Well, my studio has the best Apogee converters money can buy." Sure, the occasional gearhead will get excited—just as you do—for that latest piece of audio gadgetry, but most will just want simple reassurance that you're able to make a current-sounding recording.

- **Auto-Tune.** Most clients today expect the pitch-correcting abilities of Auto-Tune to be available in a professional-grade studio. Antares Auto-Tune is one of the most sought-after pieces of software in any studio, and it's not too expensive to buy. Frequently used to simply tighten up vocal passages or static instruments, Auto-Tune has become one of those utilities that when overused produces a sound that—while cringe-worthy for most audiophiles—has become extremely popular. While I don't like abusing

Auto-Tune, my clients seem to love it and given current recording trends, who am I to argue?

- **Compression.** High-quality compression, and using it wisely, has been a hallmark of professional studios as opposed to amateur operations. For the last few years, getting really high-quality compressors has involved a lot of analog outboard gear, which wasn't always easily compatible with high-tech digital systems. Now, many of these companies are offering extremely accurate virtual models of their analog gear. With these high-quality compressors available from Waves, SSL, API, and many others in convenient, inexpensive plug-in form, there's no excuse not to load up your plug-in suite with as many as you can get your hands on. A few extremely nice outboard compressors can help, too, because they can be patched directly into your signal chain.

- **Microphones.** Another area where home studios generally fall short is the availability of high-quality recording microphones. This can be your studio's area to shine. Even with a modest investment, you can have great microphones that easily beat out anything a budget bedroom operation will have.

- **Acoustic treatment.** As we talked about earlier, part of a studio's charm is how good it sounds. One reason people use commercial studios even with the introduction of high-quality home recording systems is that there's a lot of investment, both in terms of time and money, to make a recording room sound good. Keeping a chunk of your budget devoted to achieving acoustic perfection in your recording space will help you keep up with your clients' expectation that the work done in your space surpasses their own.

Aside from this, staying current on how commercial recordings evolve is another very important aspect of this business. While I consider myself very diverse in the kind of music that I enjoy, I don't listen to a lot of Top 40 pop music or rap. Still, I do have clients coming in wanting to record in both of these styles, and it's my duty to remain familiar. While we all have our personal tastes in music, consider keeping a small library of industry classics in genres you don't particularly care for.

Standing Out: Professional Certifications

Whenever I meet with a lawyer or doctor for the first time, I usually take the time to check out his or her credentials—and the Internet has made this all too easy.

However, audio engineers are typically judged solely on the merit of their best-sounding project—the ears of a paying client are always the bottom line that determines whether or not a project ultimately moves forward. Since a degree or certification of any kind is not necessarily a prerequisite for being a top-notch studio engineer, professional certifications aren't necessarily the first things you should think about spending your budget on. If you've got the chops, let your clients' ears—rather than your certificates of achievement—do the deciding. Once you've started establishing yourself, taking the time and money to become certified in certain aspects of your studio operations is a great way to maintain high standards.

Professional certifications offer a few things that even the best self-taught engineers can benefit from:

- The ability to be listed on the certifying organization's website as a certified engineer
- An in-depth look at the shortcuts and built-in features of any good recording software package
- Staying current with trends in the music industry by engaging with trainers who are professional engineers themselves

But what if your knowledge is somewhat limited going into it? Professional certification programs can help prepare you for almost every aspect of your job, but it's still going to take both a keen sense of audio engineering and music production in general to pull off recording for paying clients. Even the best certification programs still rely on the fact that you've got the basics of the job down.

The most popular programs are run by companies such as AVID (who certifies Pro Tools operators and experts directly) and Berklee College of Music, which is a world-class music college that offers online instruction. Both cost plenty of money, but you'll learn some great skills that will help recording sessions go smoother (and maybe, just maybe, help your clients sound a little better).

That being said, some online certification programs aren't worth the paper they're printed on. Many online sites will regurgitate information that you've already seen on other web resources, and offer very little in the way of personal, one-on-one instruction. A simple web certificate of completion is not a certification. Certifying yourself in software, hardware, or methodology takes a lot of hard, hands-on work to show that you know what you're doing. When looking at a training course, one thing is most important: the actual hands-on time you'll get with the equipment. If you won't be actively learning how to record and mix, then it's not a good place for you.

Recording Schools

While we're talking about certification, a note about recording schools, including those that offer nondegree diplomas in recording or audio technology: Many of these schools have a relatively bad reputation among professional audio engineers, and with good reason. Several of them operate in a fashion that doesn't give the individual enough hands-on time, and as any good engineer will tell you, being hands-on with your equipment is the only way to truly learn the science behind audio engineering.

Many of these schools offer programs that range from four to six months of time, and cost upward of $15,000. While there are perfectly legitimate schools that have audio engineering programs, you might want to ask a few important questions before trying to polish your skills and credibility with a recording school diploma:

- How much hands-on time does each student get with the equipment in a productive, live session? You should have at least five hours of hands-on time per week, if not more.
- What professional industry-recognized certifications come along with the diploma program?
- What are the credentials of the instructors and staff?
- Is the equipment I'll be learning on state of the art?
- Does the program explain the basics of audio engineering—including signal flow, gain, and all the gritty electrical details that make things work?

12 After Recording: Helping Clients to the Finish Line

As any good audio engineer knows, getting your client's recording and mixing project finished is only half of what's required to put out a retail-ready project. There is still the mastering, packaging, and distribution to be done. It's up to you to decide if you're up for the challenge of offering these extra services to your clients; of course, it's nice to have additional income, but if you can't do these things well enough to make your customers extremely happy, it's not worth the bad reviews that come from offering a subpar product. Being a quality resource for your clients involves doing what you do better than any of your competition. If you get yourself involved in a segment of your business you don't quite understand, it can do way more harm than good.

As scary as that sounds, if you've got the resources, time, and talent to offer after-recording services to your clients, go for it! Being a comprehensive resource can be great, especially for projects on limited budgets, which would benefit from having extra services thrown in.

Let's look at some of these extras that you could potentially offer from your recording studio business. Ask yourself the following questions:

- Do you have special skills outside of recording and mixing?
- Is there time in your schedule for additional projects, or do you need to dedicate most of your time to mixing and recording?
- Are extra services such as graphic design and audio mastering available in your community? If they're not, consider offering these as a way to fill a missing market—just don't overwhelm yourself in the process.

Mastering: In-House or Outsourcing?

The final step in any good recording is mastering, the all-important combination of level matching, equalization, and compression that gives your mix that extra "pop." Mastering puts the finishing touches on your final recording; most clients' work won't be complete without this important step. A good mastering job can mean the difference between a song getting airplay—and standing out amongst the competition—or not. It's such an important step that you need to carefully consider whether or not to offer this service directly to your clients, or consider outsourcing to another studio.

The benefits of keeping things in-house are mainly financial, but there's also an element of being able to have total control over your clients' project, from start to finish. It's an extra service you can throw in, whether as part of the original package estimate or as an additional paid service, either bundled with recording services or as a stand-alone service for projects not recorded in your studio. Keep in mind, though, that a good mastering engineer has access to many tools that you may not, even with an extensive digital recording setup.

There's also one huge advantage to outsourcing your mastering: a fresh pair of ears.

We talked earlier about how your ears are your most valuable asset in your recording studio. Think about the ear fatigue that comes with working in your studio during a typical session, and that'll easily put the other issue into perspective. You've just spent weeks, maybe months, and in extreme cases, over a year with one client and their material. You've heard these same songs so many times and know them inside and out. Sounds like a great reason to master it yourself, right? Think again. Your ears need a break. A good mastering engineer trims the actual mix so there's very little dead space at the beginning and end (however appropriate to the aesthetic of the song), and also makes sure each song flows with others on the album. However, the most important thing a mastering engineer brings to the project is the ability to listen to the material with an objective of finding ways to improve the overall sound of the mix, without changing the content itself. This is really, really hard if you've been listening to the same mixes on your own system for a long time, and especially hard when you've come to an agreement with yourself and your client that the final mixes are "final." Handing the mixes off to a good mastering engineer makes the whole process a lot smoother, and gives way for someone with a new perspective to help you, and your client, make the product the best it can be.

But let's say you do decide to offer mastering in-house. I'm going to assume you have a good grasp of the concepts that go into mastering, such as leveling, compressing, and EQing a final mix. Without a very thorough understanding of the processes it takes to go from a rough mix to a polished end product, you won't be a good mastering engineer—don't feel bad, there are some amazing mastering engineers who aren't good mix engineers—and you won't be able to offer anything worthwhile to your client.

In order to offer top-notch mastering, you should make sure you have equipment that's suited for the job. Most good mastering houses start by using high-quality digital-to-analog conversion, which takes the digital signal from your mixing setup (that's assuming you're all digital) in the highest resolution possible (usually 24-bit, 192-kHz, if not 24-bit, 96-kHz), and uses high-quality algorithms to convert that signal into a pure analog signal. From there, the analog signal is used to feed outboard compression and equalization and then brought back into the digital realm with analog-to-digital conversion, where it's edited on a linear two-track editor.

Many mastering houses don't go all out with the analog rig, though. There's perfectly good mastering being done on all-digital, in-the-box systems as well. It takes a special knowledge of the process of mastering—and how to milk every available amount of volume out of the master while clarifying and balancing the frequency spectrum—to be able to master in-the-box, just as it does being on the outboard side of things. Offering mastering in-the-box is a lot easier and a lot cheaper, but still takes lots of skill.

If you feel this type of equipment is a good investment for you (it might be, you might even go the extra step and decide to just open as a mastering business, with your entire business focused solely on mastering as opposed to tracking and mixing), then go for it. It's always nice to have the ability to master projects yourself, but just remember that if your primary business is tracking and mixing, having access to a fresh pair of ears is invaluable when you start the mastering stage.

Packaging and Artwork

Any time a client gets ready to sell a commercial release of any type, there's going to be a need for artwork. Unless you have superior graphic design skills, this is an area where your clients will most likely need to outsource production. Artwork can be extremely expensive to produce, and rightfully so. It takes a lot of talent and a lot of time to produce clear, concise artwork for items as small as CD inserts. Of course, if your graphic design skills are up to par—or you can partner with a local graphic designer to provide the service to you at a wholesale price—you can offer this in-house. Most clients will need a minimum of an album cover—called "cover art," but depending on their budget and intended distribution method, they might want to have a full package designed for both retail and digital distribution (many of the finer digital distribution services allow you to upload full cover and booklet artwork for download with the album).

Just as with mastering, the benefits of doing this in-house are mainly financial and might be more hassle than they're worth. If you can find a local partner willing to work with you for a price that benefits everybody involved, it's a great thing to add on. You might, as we mentioned before, be able to start offering package deals to your clients, giving them a mastered, finished product ready for store shelves. Otherwise, remember that taking on more than you can reasonably manage can actually be more harmful to your business than anything else.

Digital Distribution

Perhaps the hottest development of the last few years in the music business has been digital distribution.

Standard record companies have always made a large chunk of their money on physical media sales, whether on vinyl, cassette, or CD. This was traditionally a profitable avenue for the big record companies, although not so much for the artists themselves unless they were selling millions of units, and even then, only if the record deal was negotiated strategically. For indie artists, it's always been a badge of honor to have their own physical products to sell, whether the endeavor was actually profitable or not. For many music listeners, having the physical product to open and enjoy will always be a priority, so many clients will still pursue physical distribution, along with digital distribution.

Download Demand

Still don't think digital distribution is for your clients? Think again. No matter how old-school, their fans may still want to buy their work online. In fact, it's been said that the amount of downloads iTunes sells doubles every 34 days. That's a lot of downloads!

I remember the feeling of buying a brand new cassette (remember those?) or CD, and being so excited to own the tangible product in my hand. Buying music used to be all about a physical product; designing, packaging, and distributing a hard copy of the work became the most important post-recording element to a recording's retail success. Getting your music into the hands of physical distributors was the holy grail of independent artists.

Now, everybody's got an iPod in their pocket. Fewer people are buying music in physical form than ever before—and that's assuming they're buying it at all. Musicians are losing a lot of money to music piracy, and it's only a given that most of your clients' projects will end up being transferred among friends in MP3 format. Considering the likelihood of somebody wanting your client's album in MP3 format, having your music accessible to the most popular digital distribution sites—iTunes Music Store, emusic, AmazonMP3, and others—is a great idea.

What makes digital distribution easy is being able to control where, when, and how your work is released to the world. Apple's iTunes Music Store is, at the time of this writing, the world's largest digital distribution resource, with over 11 million songs available for purchase, and growing by the day. Being sold on the iTunes Music Store is arguably the most convenient and well-known form of digital distribution, but unless you're a major label or indie label with lots of credibility (which generally comes in the form of being a major imprint), you'll have to do business with a third-party intermediary in order to get your work sold on iTunes. This is unfortunate, but doing business with Apple's iTunes distribution has been made purposefully difficult, mainly to help maintain a standard of quality throughout the store. As an engineer, can you imagine if thousands of independent artists were allowed to directly upload their content for sale without oversight of trained entities? Think about that, and it all makes sense.

So let's say your client has a final product, and they'd like to release it through digital distribution outlets. Accomplishing this is relatively easy, and it's a process that you can help with, armed with some simple knowledge.

Many sites—such as TuneCore, SongCast, and CD Baby—will act as this intermediary for a small fee. Each service does things differently, but they're all offering the same thing: to verify your content, prepare it for sale, and upload it to the digital distribution store of your choice. They then collect the royalties paid on behalf of the store and pay them to your client.

Let's use TuneCore and iTunes as our examples. TuneCore has one of the best reputations in the industry and many of my clients have been very happy customers of their services. At the time of this writing TuneCore was the largest iTunes distributor for independent musicians, with, according to their website, one TuneCore artist sold every second on iTunes.

- First, you or your client will prepare to upload the file to TuneCore. After you've signed up for an account with the service, here's where you actually upload the product that will be sold. These files will be uploaded in an uncompressed file type; it's best to use the final mastering files in 16-bit, 44.1kHz WAV format; however, you can rip the file from a CD or other media, as long as it's clean and without any skips or jumps. The actual mastering files from the session do work better.
- TuneCore collects a fee from the client for acting as the intermediary; this is generally in the $45 range, per album.
- TuneCore assembles the digital information, including all necessary ID3 tagging information and cover art, and uploads it to the iTunes Music Store.
- When an iTunes Music Store user buys a song or an entire album, Apple pays TuneCore a preset rate. While iTunes Music Store can set the price at whatever they wish—one penny or a hundred dollars—you'll receive 70 cents per song and $7 per album.
- TuneCore pays your client this money directly without taking any money for themselves. Other distributors vary in their policies, but TuneCore favors an upfront fee with no perpetual royalties.

According to TuneCore, once an album is submitted to iTunes Music Store, it goes live within around twenty-four hours.

Storing Client Masters

If there's one necessary part of any recording studio, it's storage. I'm not talking about a room for your spare equipment or cables—I'm talking about digital storage. While it's true that digital storage space has gotten dirt cheap in the last few years, it's still a finite resource in most recording studios.

After your client's work is completed (and paid for in full), it's time to turn over the master finished copy of the work, usually in data format. I will usually provide two copies—a 24-bit, 96-kHz version for mastering, and a 16-bit, 44.1-kHz copy for listening. What you decide to offer your clients is up to you, but this is a combination that generally works for me. From there, with the tracking and mixing stages completed, you'll find yourself with lots of hard drive space taken up by your clients' work. Depending on the software package you used to record and mix the project, you may have several gigs' worth of session data, edits, overdubs, and mixes. The final disposition of these files is something your studio will have to deal with.

Why is this data important? Sometimes clients need to access their session data after the fact. Some will want to do remixes with other producers or engineers, and some might want to come back at a later date and add more elements to the recording, for example if they get a windfall and are able to afford to "perfect" things even more. (Ever wonder why some popular bands re-release their albums once they get signed? More money equals more money to polish things even further!) Many studios handle this differently; some require their clients to purchase an external hard drive that can be used to store the session exclusively and then becomes property of the band, including the session, after the work is completed. Others will store on hard drive servers or other media (such as DVD-R disks) for a predetermined period of time.

How long you store your clients' masters is up to you. I generally notify all clients in writing that I'm willing to store their masters for one year from the date they receive the finished product. If you've got the space and resources to store them longer, then it's fine to offer different terms—or not store them at all. It's your call. I generally do not provide my clients full Pro Tools session files of their work unless specifically requested. You may wish to do things differently, but I prefer to keep the files intact and untouched in case the client decides to come back at a later date for remixing or touch-ups; you don't need people to have messed with the session, causing potential compatibility problems for you down the line.

13 Business Endgame

We've come to the end of this book and hopefully you're headed in the right direction for opening your home-based recording studio business. You've worked very hard to get to this point and for that you should be extremely proud. Now, let's talk about the endgame of your business—how to prepare yourself for the future (hopefully a long, profitable career as a recording engineer).

If your business is meeting its break-even point every month and evolving steadily to be able to generate a small profit, then you're in great shape. From here it's about maintaining your standards and giving your clients the best repeat experiences you possibly can. If your business isn't meeting its basic needs, and costing you time, money, and resources that you don't have, you should start considering the other option—closing up shop.

When you're caught up in the adrenaline-fueled few months of starting a brand new business, it's hard to ever think about closing down your business. For one reason or another, your business may indeed fail. That's alright—small businesses have a high rate of failure, especially in today's roller coaster of an economy.

You've given it a good shot—and whether you found success beyond your wildest dreams or frustration and disappointment that you've never felt before (maybe both), you can rest assured that you've given your all and however far you made it was all due to your hard work, hustle, and good luck. Now that you've worked with your business in a way that you're proud of, it's time to look at the endgame of your recording studio. Whether that means shutting down operations and moving on to the next adventure in your life or stepping up the game and working with bigger and better clients, you'll need to be prepared.

Repeat Business

Recording studios thrive on repeat business. It's no secret that the best studios have had multiple visits by their top-grossing clients. While many of your clients, at least at first, won't be going multiplatinum, repeat business by even the most low-budget client is welcome and a necessary part of having a successful studio. When your clients look at the work you've done, the best possible scenario is one where they feel that they as a band have gotten to where they are today with your help in shaping their sound.

While it's always necessary for your business to evolve to naturally suit your clients' needs in this ever-changing industry, you still have to maintain high standards of both product and customer service in order to maintain your client base for a long time. It's a simple concept, one that's the same in any business, but it's especially important in the fickle music industry where many institutions—be they studios, instrument shops, or live performance venues—tend to get by with a complacent swagger once they hit a stride of success. Repeat business in the studio industry can easily be yours by offering a quality product and exceptional service.

So what else can you do to make sure your clients come back for more, money in hand? Setting yourself apart by offering unique gear and extra services is always a plus. Most important, produce a good product and make sure your clients know where to find you. Keeping in touch with your clients—and offering moral support for their hard-earned careers in the music business—can keep them on your side. As their careers grow, keeping them close and included in your circle of clients can help you grow professionally and financially as well. Many engineers and producers have found great success this way.

Wholesale Time

Sometimes, you might find that you've outgrown your studio for a certain project. You might need to consider outsourcing time at a larger local or regional facility to meet your clients' needs. While I always considered my studio big enough for just about everything, I once had a project that required tracking two drum kits simultaneously—and honestly, it really did sound as cool as you might think! However, I needed a lot more space to make this happen, and one of my local studios was able to help.

Finding a local studio you can partner with as a freelance engineer is really important, and maintaining a positive relationship can help in a pinch.

Reach out to your local studios and find out if they offer a rate for a freelance engineer—make it clear you'll be engineering the session yourself, and if they're willing (and you know the equipment), they may not charge you to have a studio engineer of their own with you. In my case, my local studio—after checking my references, many of which were mutual friends of the studio owner—offered me a key and an alarm access code with instructions to simply leave a check whenever my sessions were over. You may not get so lucky, especially if you've not got an established reputation as a bulletproof engineer. You may end up having to pay for one of their engineers to be your assistant, to oversee your operation of their equipment and to ensure their gear will be taken care of properly. Either way, the cost to rent time at another studio facility is well worth it and instantly allows your capabilities to expand far outside your home studio.

Here are some scenarios that might require you to outsource a project:

- Your live room will not fit the necessary instruments or ensembles.
- The equipment you have isn't what the client wants, i.e., some clients may request certain preamps or compressors for a signature vocal tone.
- A conflict in your home prevents the full use of your space (or distraction-free use of your space).
- Renting gear for a certain project (microphones, outboard equipment, converters) is more cost prohibitive than renting the full facility.

This is also another example of why making your studio industry-standard compatible is extremely important. Most professional studios will be running Pro Tools; many will also use Logic, but any studio worth their hourly rate will be offering Pro Tools in their tracking rooms. You'll be able to record your session there and seamlessly return to your studio for mixing and overdubs—easily expanding your capabilities outside your studio (and budget).

If you do partner with a larger facility to buy wholesale recording time for your clients, keep in mind a couple simple rules. It's the same courtesy you would expect if you opened your studio to other engineers.

- Respect all house rules. This includes rules on SPL limits, guests in the studios, alcohol, food, and drink.
- Treat their equipment as you would want yours treated. The cost of this type of gear is still fresh in your mind, I'm sure, and you know what kind of liabilities the studio has in opening their control room to you.

Your Standard of Quality

As we talked about earlier, maintaining good relationships with your clients involves a great number of things, including keeping up your standards of quality under every circumstance. Letting quality of product slip is the kiss of death for many businesses in the service industry and recording studios are no exception. Your reputation will depend on the end product being something that your clients can use commercially with success.

What's the most important thing to remember to maintain your standard of quality? It's about pacing yourself. It may take awhile—although some businesses are far luckier than others—but once you reach a point where you're booking frequent sessions, you need to make sure you're not overextending your reach. Even if you hire employees—and that's not an expense you should be considering if you're still relatively new—you'll need to make sure they don't overwork themselves either. Fatigue—both physical and mental—can lead to sloppy mixes and botched tracking sessions, which in turn generates unhappy clientele. While it may be attractive to overwork yourself for a bigger paycheck, you'll lose way more business in the future if you botch important projects.

Ongoing Royalties

If you've stepped into a producing role for your clients, you might be entitled to ongoing royalties. This isn't something that is likely to happen until you're working with major- or indie-label bands with a large following and commercial potential, but it's a very common situation once you've reached that point.

Negotiating royalties is something best left to a talented entertainment lawyer. It's a tangle of very intricate issues that you won't have the knowledge and experience to navigate yourself, no matter how good you feel at the moment. As with all contracts, make sure a qualified attorney that you trust has helped you negotiate your percentage. It's better for everybody involved if things are kept within legal boundaries and dealt with professionally.

So let's say you're working as a producer with an artist who's being signed to a label. After your actual recording expenses are paid (which is generally written into the artist's initial contract and is part of the artist's advance from the label), you'll be getting paid royalties. You may also be entitled to a producer's advance against your future royalties, which will be paid up front as well. As a start-up in the music recording business, you can realistically expect to be offered a small percentage—between

1 and 3 percent—as your producer's royalty. This is paid against the suggested retail pricing of the final product and will be sent to you on a quarterly or yearly basis, depending on the terms of the contract.

Of course this isn't something you'll need to worry about at first, unless you get very lucky. As your business moves forward, and you as an engineer and producer become a much more bulletproof brand, you could see a percentage of your income generated from ongoing royalties, even after you're no longer in business. As long as the band is selling the material, you'll get your percentage.

Knowing When to Quit

Nobody likes to think about jumping ship on a new business, but it's an unfortunate reality that sometimes even the best plans don't work out. I won't go into a lot of great detail, but do yourself a huge favor: Know when to quit. Everybody's heard the statistics about the number of small businesses that fail, and I know it's not encouraging. The numbers vary wildly depending on what survey you're reading at the moment, but a general statistic is that 50 percent of small businesses fail within the first five years. In all honesty, nobody—not even the most seasoned business veteran—can predict a business's survival or failure. The only way to find out is to do your best and see what happens.

Unfortunately, you also have to accept the realities of running a recording studio.

Let's be pessimistic for a moment: One major thing to realize is that you're in a very small niche business. Your potential client base is relatively limited, especially if you're located in a smaller community. Not everyone who plays music needs a recording—a lot of cover bands get by only on the strength of their live performances and don't intend to release anything commercially—and only a percentage of those that record will require your services as a professional engineer. You're in a business that's supported by clients who generally don't make a lot of money in the beginning stages of their career, and a lot of things can happen that might keep clients from being able to afford your services.

If you can't support yourself and your business on the income you have coming in, it might be time to consider closing down. You made a good effort and that's all you could ever ask of yourself. Don't take it personally—the odds may have been stacked against you from the beginning. Even if you have a good product, there may be other factors working against you that you can't control. And that's not saying you can't go back to your full-time job and still take freelance clients on the side when time permits.

Selling Your Studio: Equipment versus Business

If things don't work out as you had planned, it's not that you necessarily are a failure; sometimes your business is just ahead of its time, or there's way too much established competition in your region. I know it hurts to close a business; I've done it in the past and seen others do it, too. Don't feel like a failure, though. Keep it in perspective: Even if things didn't work out, you still gave it your best effort and did something that many people only dream of doing. That's something to be proud of, no matter the end result.

So if it comes time to sell your business, there are two things to keep in mind. Are you selling the business itself, or just the equipment you've used to do your work? It's a big difference, because there's a different value on each item.

If you're selling the actual business, it's going to be tough to figure out exactly how much to attempt to charge. Chances are, you're not selling your business because you made too much money and don't need to work anymore. As a recording studio, your biggest asset, after your equipment, will be your knowledge, and without you at the helm, any future incarnation of your business may not be what you had in mind. Think about this before trying to sell your business as a whole.

If you're selling your equipment, keep in mind that recording gear, in good condition, maintains a relatively good value, especially items such as microphones and outboard gear, equipment that can be used no matter how advanced tracking systems become in the future. A good indicator of value is eBay; when selling used gear, I generally average the recently sold prices on eBay and find a good price based on the value of items in similar condition.

Finding an outlet for selling gear is not difficult. Your local Craigslist site is a great place to start; face-to-face dealings generally have less hassle and much faster payment. From there, consider trying gear-trading message boards with a specific following of professional engineers. You'll be dealing with other engineers who know the value of what you're selling and can do an easy, limited-haggling transaction with someone who isn't lost on how the gear itself works.

Letting Go

Watching my parents close their antique-dealing business after several years of giving it their best was extremely hard, and an experience I'll never forget. Closing your business is so incredibly difficult, sometimes harder than opening one, since you aren't powered by the rush of hope and expectation. It's a grieving process almost akin to the death of a close friend or family member. You've built your world around running a business that you've loved, and I know how difficult it is once you've ingrained that business into your identity. But if you're losing money hand over fist and can't support yourself or your business with the revenue you've been bringing in, it's probably time to consider closing your business. If you're having doubts about whether your business is truly sustainable any longer, look back on the business plan we worked on in chapter 3.

- Are you meeting your break-even point?
- How badly in debt are you compared to your original plan?
- Are your personal finances strained by your business debts and shortcomings?
- Do you have a second form of income to sustain yourself and the business while you work on further developing the business?
- How likely are you to meet your break-even point with the current selection of clients in your market, assuming you work with a reasonable percentage of them?

Earlier we talked about going full or part time. If your business is steadily failing to meet your basic needs, then you should consider dropping down to part time first. If your business can't be sustained at that level, then you should consider closing the doors. It's hard to swallow lost investments and lost time. The good news is that you've built very valuable experience, whether you open your own business again or go to work for another studio. True, the lost money can be a huge burden, too, especially if the business didn't have the ability to pay back your initial loans as you expected. For that reason, you might be tempted to hang on, even at a potential loss. You'll feel so much better about this emotionally draining decision if you prioritize—realizing that your sanity helps greatly in the long run if you make a graceful exit before the liabilities of a failing business overwhelm you, personally and professionally.

That being said, be proud of yourself. If you're reading this part of the book after you've given it your best shot, that's all you can ask of yourself. Be proud; you've taken a serious stab at your dreams. Just because this one didn't work out doesn't mean that your next one won't. And, most importantly, don't be afraid to follow your dreams again—you never know where they might take you, and your next adventure might truly be the secret to your success.

Appendix A:
Resources on the Web

Running a Small Business

Here are a couple of great resources for starting—and running—your small business. There are a lot of really confusing websites out there, but I always reference these two; I mainly trust these resources because they're run exclusively by the federal government. They're not trying to sell you anything; they just have good information to share.

The United States Small Business Administration
www.sba.gov

Small Business and Self-Employed Tax Center
www.irs.gov/businesses/small/index.html

Recording and Audio Engineering Links

The Internet is a great place to not only network, but to stay on top of your chosen field. Audio engineering is one of those industries that is dominated by some really smart people, and I've always found that I enjoy learning from them. Here are some great links that I find valuable during every project.

Audio Engineering Society
www.aes.org

GearSlutz.com—Gear and Studio Message Board
www.gearslutz.com/board

HomeRecording.com—Message Board
www.homerecording.com

Home Recording at About.com
http://homerecording.about.com

Pro Audio Space—Social-Networking Site for Audio Engineers
www.proaudiospace.com

ProSoundWeb—Resources for Studios and Live Audio Engineers
www.prosoundweb.com

Professional Audio Retailers

Finding good people to buy from is sometimes hard. Any Internet search will pull up thousands of retailers all competing for a piece of your studio's budget. Here are some dealers that I've worked with personally; while I'm not endorsing any one retailer, I know that many other engineers have also had positive experiences with these outlets.

American Musical Supply
www.americanmusical.com

AudioLines
www.audiolines.com

Sweetwater
www.sweetwater.com

Musician's Friend
www.musiciansfriend.com

Appendix B:
Home Studio Survival Guide

Hopefully by now, your home-based recording studio business is off and running. Maybe you've taken your first (or second, or third) paid client; maybe you've just hooked up the last piece of gear and you're waiting for the phone to ring to start selling studio time. Either way, I'm guessing you've put a lot of hard work into it at this point. Be proud! I'm sure you're working hard, but as we talked about before, the rewards of being your own boss are limitless.

But even with all that in-depth knowledge of the recording studio business that you've acquired throughout both this book and your own research, problems do happen. Recording studios, like any other technical, service-based business, are prone to technical gremlins which can lead to downtime—and thus lost profits.

In this appendix, let's talk about some common things you might need to know—call it a survival guide, a handful of worst-case-scenarios that we audio engineers face when the going gets tough.

Recovering from Data Loss

Have you ever had your hard drive crash, and in the process, lose a great amount of data? Sure, it's one of the worst things that can happen to anyone in this digital age we're living in—losing your documents, photos, and other media—but what about when your hard drive contains material from a client that's paying you, and you need it back right away?

I've been in your shoes. Imagine this: A night before a final mixing session for a project that's lasted close to a year and my hard drive decides to die. Thankfully, all I lost was my plug-ins and a handful of documents; the band's session files were all backed up to an external hard drive.

Keeping good backups is your first line of defense against data loss. Hard drive space is cheap, so you've got no excuse to run daily backups of client material. But what if you've ignored all of the advice telling you to back up regularly, and you've had a storage failure?

If it looks like your computer's hard drive has failed, check to see if it's your computer hardware or the storage device itself. Sometimes, problems that look like hard drive failure can actually be a symptom of something more serious (or, less serious, depending on how much money you stand to lose if your storage system fails during a paid project). If it's just your computer, you can easily swap out your storage device into another functioning machine. If it's not your machine, things can quickly get complicated (and expensive). Once you've determined that you've had a storage failure, it's important to act quickly.

Data recovery services are your best option if you can afford it, and the data is important enough to recover. Data recovery services take your hard drive into a clean-room environment and extract the data from the platters of the hard drive and place it onto a new, functional drive. This service can run upwards of $500 or more, but it's worth every penny to get back an once-in-a-lifetime session.

If you're on a limited budget, sometimes the best thing to do is simply eat the cost and time involved in re-tracking if only one project is lost—it'll cost you far less than an expensive data recovery service. Your time, while valuable, is a lot easier to spend than money you don't have.

iLok and You

Earlier we talked about software piracy, and how it affects the recording studio industry. Paying for your software is the honest, responsible, and correct thing to do; you're supporting a great industry, and in turn, you'll have the support you need if your essential software goes down during an important session.

Most software packages will require use of an iLok USB key. The iLok is an ingenious little device that plugs into your USB port, and essentially acts to unlock the anti-piracy features in software packages that use it. Buying one of these $40 keys is essential for all studios, since all the major plug-ins require it. You download your authorized licenses onto the iLok, and simply keep it inserted into your USB port while working. It could not be easier and it's portable, allowing you to use your licenses in other studios. That being said, the iLok can become a huge pain if you lose or damage it. You'll be required to buy a replacement, and work with your manufacturers to get new licenses deposited into your iLok account, a process that can take weeks.

Protecting your iLok is extremely important. Always keep track of it, and make sure it's attached to your computer and accounted for if your computer moves locations. Also, iLok ingeniously allows you to buy something called "zero downtime" support, which allows you instant access to backup licenses and will replace a defective iLok for you quickly. This is something you'll really appreciate having if the worst happens—and believe me, it does. I once had to put off a paying project for close to four weeks while I worked out license issues with a plug-in company who I needed to finish the mix!

A List of Spares

Now that you've got the basics of running a studio out of the way, it's time to go shopping for some spare parts, if you've got the money. Earlier, we talked about some must-have accessories; now, let's talk about some items you really need to have sitting idle as backups in case the worst happens. And while it seems highly unlikely, believe me—having spares around never hurts.

First, don't worry if you didn't budget money for these items. They're not immediately necessary, and can always be purchased as you go along. However, keep in mind that downtime during a major project is not only embarrassing but will cost you money in the end—and getting spare parts is certainly insurance against this happening. Before beginning a major project with a high-paying client, it makes a lot of sense to check all your equipment and the backups as well.

Here's a short checklist of backup items you may find helpful to keep around. Don't make a common mistake and get caught without a plan B when it really counts—plan ahead!

- Long XLR Cables
- Interconnects (1/4", XLR)
- Spare iLok Key
- Spare Headphones
- Headphone Cables
- Digital Connectors (S/PDIF, optical)
- Extra Microphone Stands and Clamps

■ Backup copies of your operating system and all other software you use, updated regularly.

Choosing a Microphone

One of the most common queries I get from aspiring recording engineers involves understanding the difference between the many types of microphones available to them. If you're new to using microphones, don't be surprised if you're confused, too!

There are three main types of microphones that you'll encounter in the studio: condenser, dynamic, and ribbon. Condenser microphones are powered by phantom power, and tend to be the top choice for vocals, acoustic instruments, drum overheads, and anything that requires you to achieve a flat, uniform frequency response with fine detail. Dynamic microphones offer typically less detailed of a sound signature on the higher frequencies, but tend to react extremely well to high-SPl environments, especially amplifiers and drums. Ribbon microphones are either dynamic or phantom-powered, and offer exceptional detail with a somewhat limited frequency response, but sound incredible anywhere a dynamic microphone would—especially amps and vocals.

From there, you have the option of large-diaphragm or small-diaphragm. Small diaphragm mics work very well on instruments, whereas large-diaphragm

Still need help? Here's a quick guide you can reference.

Type of Mic	Example	Suggested Use
Condenser	AKG C414, Oktava MC012	Vocals (more accurate sound), Acoustic Instruments, Live Recording
Dynamic	Shure SM57, Heil PR-30	Vocals (for a more rock sound), Amplifiers, Close Drums
Ribbon	Cascade Fathead II, Nady RSM-4	Guitar Amp, Acoustic Guitar (in pairs)

microphones shine on vocals. There's no hard-or-fast rule on which you can use for what purpose—just find something that works to your ears' liking, and go with it!

Taking Care of Microphones

Microphones are sensitive creatures. They're expensive, relatively fragile, and absolutely indispensable in the studio. Taking good care of your expensive microphones is really, really important and I can't stress it enough. I've lost plenty of time because of poorly-maintained microphones causing problems at other studios and it's encouraged me to work extra hard to take care of mine.

Microphones are generally very sensitive to moisture, so the best thing to do is clean your microphones after every use with a soft, dry cloth or brush. If you want to take it a step further, there's a fantastic product that I use called Microphome—it's a microphone cleaning and sanitizing foam that's specially designed to keep microphones in top working order without damaging their delicate internal parts.

You might also find that a regular, monthly cleaning with an electronics de-oxidizer helps keep the XLR connectors on your microphones working in top form. Frequently, microphones are prone to clicks, pops, and cracks because the XLR connector becomes dirty and oxidized, creating a loss of signal. Keeping this area cleaned will also minimize these embarrassing episodes while in the heat of tracking.

Another thing to watch out for is to not apply phantom power to microphones that don't need it, especially ribbon microphones. While the chances are remote (and most new ribbon microphones are either phantom-powered or phantom-protected), you can still cause some serious damage if you apply phantom power to a microphone that doesn't need it. Keep this in mind when patching.

Index

About the Author

Joe Shambro is an audio engineer, music producer, and music technology writer from St. Louis, MO. He has worked exclusively as a freelance engineer with a successful home-based recording and mixing studio, as well as traveling worldwide as an in-demand live sound engineer, mixing concerts and recording live for major-label and independent clients.

As a recording engineer, he has recorded a diverse portfolio of projects for musicians, corporate, and government clients, from a concert in a bomb-proof bunker at the US Embassy in Amman, Jordan, recording tree frogs in rural Iowa, and capturing the deafening roar of a Space Shuttle launch up-close in high-definition.

Joe is also a home recording & music technology writer for The New York Times Company's About.com property, as well as a contributing writer for EQ Magazine. His work has been featured on many media outlets, including CNN, The Armed Forces Network, and Clear Channel Radio.

KNACK® MAKE IT EASY

Look for these Knack titles that bring you fast-reading, highly visual, how-to books!

AVAILABLE TITLES

Cooking
Calorie Counter Cookbook
Canning, Pickling & Preserving
Chicken Classics
Chinese Cooking
College Cookbook
Diabetes Cookbook
Fabulous Desserts
Fish & Seafood Cookbook
Gourmet Cooking on a Budget
Grilling Basics
Indian Cooking
Italian Cooking
Low-Salt Cooking
Mexican Cooking
Quick & Easy Cooking
Slow Cooking
Soup Classics
South American Cooking
Thai Cooking
Vegetable Cookbook

Games
Bridge for Everyone
Chess for Everyone
Magic Tricks
Pool & Billiards

General Interest
American Sign Language
Astrology
Bartending Basics

Body Language
Digital Moviemaking
First Aid
Night Sky
Self-Defense for Women
Wine Basics

House & Home
Clean Home, Green Home
Dorm Living
Green Decorating & Remodeling
Home Repair & Maintenance
Organizing Your Home
Treehouses
Universal Design

Music
Drums for Everyone
Guitar for Everyone
Piano for Everyone

Outdoor Recreation
Canoeing for Everyone
Car Camping for Everyone
Cycling for Everyone
Fishing for Everyone
Hiking & Backpacking
Kayaking for Everyone
Knots You Need
Rock Climbing

Parenting
Baby Sign Language
Baby's First Year
Healthy Snacks for Kids
Parenting a Preschooler
Pregnancy Guide
Raising Your Toddler

Pets
Dog Care & Training
Dog Tricks
Puppies

Sports
Absolute Abs
Coaching Youth Baseball
Coaching Youth Basketball
Coaching Youth Soccer
Weight Training for Women

Wedding
Planning Your Wedding
Wedding Flowers

To order call 800-243-0495 • www.KnackBooks.com